TWAYNE'S WORLD AUTHORS SERIES
A Survey of the World's Literature

Sylvia Bowman, Indiana University
GENERAL EDITOR

INDIA

M. L. Sharma, Slippery Rock State College
EDITOR

Subramanya Bharati

(TWAS 325)

Subramanya Bharati

Subramanya Bharati

By KULDIP K. ROY

Twayne Publishers, Inc.   ::   New York

Library of Congress Cataloging in Publication Data

Roy, Kuldip K
  Subramanya Bharati.

  (Twayne's world authors series, TWAS 325)
  Bibliography: p. 151.
  1. Subrahmanya Bharati, C., 1882-1921.
PL4758.9.S8437Z85   894'.811'15   74-6411
ISBN 0-8057-2153-3

To My Parents
In reverent gratitude for having
given me a meaning and purpose of
life.

Contents

About the Author

Kuldip K. Roy (born Feb. 28, 1935), Doctor of Letters, has had a distinguished career as a literary critic, editor, poet-translator, research fellow, and historian. He is a Fellow of the Asiatic Society and the Theosophical Society and is a consulting editor of several University Presses.

Dr. Roy has published many critical articles in scholarly magazines on varied subjects ranging from multidisciplinary historical research to belles lettres and literary criticism. Among his published works are *Mirza Ghalib* (1969), *Stray Thoughts and Other Poems* (1970), *Waris Shah* (1971), *The Swami and the Comrade* (1973), and *Living My Own Death* (forthcoming).

Dr. Roy is presently engaged in a sloka by sloka translation into English verse of all variegated editions of the *Ramayana* in major Indian and South East Asian languages, which has never before been planned or done in a single project.

Preface

Subramanya Bharati is recognized as one of the foremost modern Tamil poets. He is entitled by his genius and his work to rank among those who have transcended the limitations of race, language, and country to become the universal possession of mankind.

Bharati is one of the few poets of modern India who sang during the most ardent period of his country's political growth when deliverance from foreign rule was too far away even to be seen as a speck on the horizon. It was undoubtedly on the horizon when Mahatma Gandhi entered the scene, but Bharati died when that happened. The body of national thought that he wove into song was that which preceded Gandhi; it was Vivekananda's and Dadabhai Naoroji's and Tilak's India and not that which most of the present day admirers of India's struggles may have in mind, which forms the material of Bharati's literary output.[1]

A short account of the Tamilians and their variegated literature as given in chapter 1 is necessary to appreciate Bharati's work because for over a hundred years before him, the Tamil genius had not expressed itself at its best in any department of life, much less on the creative side in song and literature. The reasons are many, both political and sociological. This was considered worth exploring, if only to liberate the stream of creative fancy from the sands of a decorous but false tradition in education and approach to life. Creative artists like Subramanya Bharati are like oases in the desert — as though the endless waste of sand gets wearied of itself and produces a spot of green for the joy of sheer reaction.

The second chapter of this book deals with Bharati's short life of thirty-nine years, full of trials and tribulations, which a freedom fighter had to face in the early years of this century. But his was "a spirit wild," which could triumph in the midst of penury and suffering. His political guru was the extremist Lokmanya Tilak, though Bharati also had the poetic insight to hail Gandhi as the redeemer and savior of India. His spiritual gurus were many, one among them being Sister Nivedita of the Ramakrishna Order.

It is the work of this remarkable poet and patriot that we study in the third chapter. Bharati's poetical genius is the happy result of a cross-fertilization, the clash and contact between two great cultures. It is said that the oyster breeds the pearl in a moment of irritation. His poems are lyrical outbursts in a like moment of conflict, suffering, and struggle revealing an almost Kalidasian touch in freshness, spontaneity, and suggestive power.

Bharati's works, their contents, and literary forms are true to Indian heritage which is the subject of the fourth chapter. Just as in the ancient days Vyasa and Valmiki served human progress and culture, this bard of Tamilnadu has served to uphold the noblest traditions of India's culture and heritage in modern times.

Subsequent chapters of this book (chapters five through eight) describe and assess Bharati's patriotic writings, religious poetry and mysticism. These are as concrete and detailed as possible. A detailed analysis of all his published and unpublished writings in English and Tamil however would be impossible in a book of this scope. This book judiciously selects his best and most popular works, briefly mentioning the rest.

This limitation to Bharati's "best and most popular" works has limited, of course, the negative criticism also. And the focus of attention on the thematic aspects of his literary output has limited technical and stylistic criticism. But the most important negative criticism of Bharati has always been directed precisely toward his "best and most popular" works. His chief critics have always attacked his religious ideas and mysticism as also his larger prose writings. The concluding chapter of this book discusses the chief criticisms of his work, and places him as one of the biggest luminaries of the twentieth century. Bharati was not only a man and a poet, he was also a deathless messenger of courage and hope.

I must end this on a more personal note and record my extreme indebtedness and a sense of obligation to Professor Mohan Lal Sharma, Editor of the Twayne India Series, whom I was able to meet once again during my recent visit to the United States on a convention. He has always been a perennial fount of inspiration and a perpetual source of guidance, and he has unfailingly encouraged me whenever I seemed to falter. My thanks are also due to Dr. Sylvia Bowman of Indiana University, General Editor of the Twayne Series and Mr. Thomas T. Beeler, Executive Editor of Twayne Publishers, Inc., for their unstinted help and support in bringing out this work. I am also thankful to eminent Tamil scholars, translators, and writers such as the late Sri C. Rajagopalachari, Dr. Prema Nandakumar, Dr. T. P. Meenakshisundaram Pillai, Prof. P. Mahadevan, Sri A. V. Subramania Aiyar, Sri M. Ramaswamy, Prof. R. S. Desikan, Prof. A. S. Raghavan, and Sri M. Bhoothalingam from whose works I have invariably quoted. My profound thanks are also due to the Government of Tamilnadu, Bharati Tamil Sangham, and Mrs. Shakuntala Bharati (the poet's daughter) for access to several published and unpublished documents by and on Bharati without which this work could never have been completed.

My especial thanks go to Sri A. Gangadharan for his help in the final stages of preparing the book for the press.

KULDIP K. ROY

Calcutta

Acknowledgments

Without the assistance of the Government of Tamilnadu, Bharati Tamil Sangham, and all Tamil scholars, translators, writers and publishers (for details of names and publications, see Preface and selected Bibliography), this work could never have been written.

My children deserve a word of praise for genuinely and valiantly trying to reduce the accustomed noise level of their daily lives a few decibels, and Vimala, my wife for so cheerfully coping with the ill-tempered churl which the writing of a book occasionally makes me. Without her helpful advice in the preparation of the manuscript, I would have long since been submerged in a sea of paper, and it was she who prevented me from galloping off in unfruitful directions.

Chronology

1882   Subramanya Bharati born on December 11 at Ettayapuram in Tirunelveli District of Tamilnadu, India.

1887   Death of mother, Lakshmi Chinnaswami Iyer.

1887 -   Schooling at Hindu College School in Tirunelveli.
1890

1893   Title of "Bharati" conferred.

1897   Married Chellammal daughter of Chellappa Iyer of Kadayam, Tamilnadu.

1898   Death of father, Chinnaswami Iyer.

1898 -   Education at Central Hindu College, Benares.
1901

1901   Passed the Allahabad University Entrance examination in the first division.

1901 -   Service under the Raja of Ettayapuram.
1904

1904   First poem "Solitude" published in Tamil in *Viveka Bhanu* of Madurai, Tamil Teacher at Setupati High School in Madurai for three months only. Assistant Editor, *Swadesmitran* (Tamil daily of Madras).

1906   Editor, *India* (Tamil daily) and *Bala Bharata* (English Weekly).

1907   Published "Our Congress Tour" after returning from Surat session of the Indian National Congress.

1908   Published first verse collection. *Swadesa Gitangal* which was dedicated to Sister Nivedita. Went in exile to Pondicherry, then a part of French India.

1909   Published second verse collection *Janma Bhoomi* also dedicated to Sister Nivedita. Started editing *India* and *Bala Bharata* from Pondicherry. Became editor of another new Tamil daily, *Vijaya*, and a weekly, *Sarvodaya*, both published from Pondicherry.

1910   Sri Aurobindo joins Bharati at Pondicherry.

1912   Wrote his three greatest works: *Kannan Pattu, Panchali Sapatham,* and *Kuyil Patu.*

1918   Back to British India to live at Kadayam and Ettayapuram.

1919   Met Mahatma Gandhi for the first time at Madras.

1920 - Assistant editor, *Swadesmitran* for the second time.
1921

1921   Died on September 12 at Madras.

CHAPTER 1

Introduction

IN the far south of India, in a strip of land some 600 miles long between the Western Ghats and the Indian Ocean, lies the home of the Tamils, known as Tamilnadu — part of the former Madras Presidency. It is recorded by commentators that for thousands of years the Tamils occupied a vast expanse of land south of Cape Comorin, extending to the continents of Australia and Africa which formed a part of the now submerged continent of Lemuria. This land was known as Tamilakam. By volcanic action Lemuria was destroyed and swept over by the waves of the Indian Ocean, and at the same time out of its depths rose up the mighty Himalayas which resulted in the present configuration of India. Scientific researches confirm this and further investigation by geologists and oceanographers show that "the tiny land whereon the Tamils now live forms one of the most ancient territories the world has ever known."[1]

The Tamils are thus an ancient race, and their civilization dates from prehistoric times. Their language is highly cultivated and well structured, and their literature is over two thousand years old. Tamil literature is vast and varied but is mostly poetry. Its prose is still in the making and is by no means as developed as its poetry. Early Tamil literature is like no other Indian literature. It consists of various anthologies of lyrics on love and heroism and bears the sole and sacred literary record of the ancient Dravidian stock of India before it was dominated by Aryan influence. Perhaps that is the reason why it stands in such sharp contrast to Sanskrit and other Sanskrit dominated languages of India. In moral tone it is far more liberal and open than Sanskrit for it reveals the touching faith in goodness a people had through the ages. "One would be perfectly justified in saying that Tamil is the only ancient language of India that bears the reflection of the life of its people and not merely the

aristocracy of its past. In this it is more akin to English literature."[2]
In ancient Tamil literature in what is popularly known as the
Sangam Period one will find the whole gamut of human experience.
"The tragic and sublime are not infrequently touched. Laughter,
though not very pronounced, is not unknown."[3] "Grammatical and
didactic works written by Jains followed this period which in the
history of Tamil literature is known as the Post Sangam Period."[4]

Thiruvalluvar also wrote his *Kural* in this period which is rightly
claimed as a world classic. It incorporates principles of universal
appeal, independent of all warring creeds and embodies great
wisdom. Subtle humor, apt imagery, forcefulness, restraint, and
dignity add to its poetic charm. "The old conventions about the
treatment of the love themes are handled in a refined way, purged of
all grossness."[5]

From the seventh to the tenth centuries Sanskrit had been
welcomed or thrust into Tamil literature, but the best Tamil writing
had always been self-reliant. Even after freely borrowing words and
ideas from Sanskrit, Tamil literature assimilated them perfectly.
One finds an unusual blending of directness with symbolism,
vividness, correctness, and freedom from overrefined speculation,
which was at that time sadly missing in Sanskrit literature or the
literatures of other Indian languages dominated by Sanskrit.

"This cultural interplay with Sanskrit was largely responsible for
Hindu religious revival in South India popularly known as the Bhakti
movement, which gave rise to devotional literature."[6] Puranic
legends rich with poetry and religious significance swept through the
land and created a sumptuous background on which literature could
work with telling effect. The first fruits of this new influence were
mystical hymns sung by Saiva and Vaishnava devotees which expressed the yearning of the finite for the infinite and the passion of
the transient for the eternal. Tamil symbolism gained new ground
and was freely used at this stage to express the ineffable by lending
local habitation and name to the Absolute. Profound philosophical
concepts were rendered into exquisite verse of a matchless simplicity.
In such poems, the earth becomes a window opening into the beyond
through which one can see vividly — an image symbolizing the
voyagings of the human spirit toward an ultimate heaven. These
Odysseys of the spirit reflect all facets of religious experience and
their very intensity makes words break into a flood of melody.

The great epic poet Kamban inherited this threefold heritage of
Sanskrit thought and philosophy, ethical leanings and simplicity as

well as the mystical symbolism and intensity of Tamil poetry of the time. By this time the Tamils had built great empires, Tamil colonies had sprung up in Bengal, in far off Malaya, Sumatra, and Java, and Tamil national life had touched the highwater mark of material prosperity and splendor. Kamban chose Rama's life as his theme and got the details of the story from Valmiki's Sanskrit epic, the *Ramayana;* but the whole story was recreated by him in Tamil, and his long epic of some 42,000 lines enshrines all that is significant in Tamil tradition and culture. He is the most learned of Tamil poets and a study of his epic shows remarkable original beauty. With a rare insight of human nature, an unfailing sense of the dramatic, a keen mind reaching out toward profound truths with ease, precision, and a diction, rich, multitoned, and singularly poetic, this bard of Tamil Ramayana has created "a spacious allegory of human life, while expressing the highest achievements of his race by justifying the ways of God to man."[7]

After Kamban came a long period of comparative poetic sterility which saw the great commentators giving birth to Tamil prose. While the commentaries of the period reveal great acuteness and scholarship, the prose in which they are written is "either a clumsy concoction of Sanskrit and Tamil or a crabbed artificial limping towards aphoristic terseness."[8]

Tamil life itself had then shrunk to mediocrity. The Muslims and then the Marathas and after them the British gained control of the land, and Tamil literature was forced to take refuge in the monastic houses of religious orders or in the courts of petty chieftains. Arid theological hair splitting, erotic vulgarity, and sensuousness had crept into it. Islamic and Christian influences over Tamil life and culture also became evident to some extent and served as a decadent check on caste fanaticism.

In the nineteenth century, the popular poet saint Jyoti Ramalinga Swami sang of, and worked on, *Samarasa* and *Sanmarga* and tried to remove the excrescent overgrowth of the intervening centuries, so that a new life from the old, pure spring might flow down to the down-trodden masses. A direct and successful offensive against existing social evils resulted in the host of schools set up by Christian missionary societies through which the Tamilians were made to see a way to literacy and free thinking. The higher caste Tamilians were so placed by the British government that they were unable to do much besides the canvassing of public opinion by references to religion and culture.

A second tremendous effect was the indirect spell which the Reformation movement of Europe cast on Tamil thought and life of the day. Men started thinking freely and liberally on the vital problem of the relationship of God and man, which spread all over the Madras Presidency like yeast through the dough, leavening the thoughts of the people. Controversy bred controversy, and if much good feeling was not promoted, in the literary field, at least, Tamil prose was set going with a swing. The ground was fertile for prose, for here men of ordinary talents could quarrel and argue and come to an understanding or misunderstanding without the need to fly to the dizzy heights of poetry.

A third and hardly less powerful influence was the sudden switch over from Tamil to English in education, introduced by Macaulay and the British government. This, one must say, badly arrested the new-found progress of Tamil. Tamil became secondary to English, as English meant education for the elite and showed them the way to the good things of life. Under English influence, the people wanted a direct, easy, and natural medium to communicate. There was thus a simultaneous attempt to rid Tamil of its heaviness and artificiality, through the cross-fertilization of fresh and foreign ideas. The Tamil renaissance was presently in full swing. But English was becoming more important. It unified the different parts of India, a thing unknown in history so far, and provided a common understanding among the elite of British India, who were thus privileged to become the leaders of the new nation in and after the Freedom Movement that was shortly to follow. "English education led the leaders to realise the dignity of the individual in the nation."[9]

With the mounting tide of nationalism early in this century, the Tamils began to look back with pride on their past and set about freeing the present from the degradation that had set in. The Freedom Movement was popularized in Madras Presidency by many forces, chiefly by Subramanya Bharati's songs. He was a poet, essayist, political journalist, translator, short-story writer, novelist — in effect, a complete and a comprehensive man of letters and wizard of the pen. His genius gave the transforming glow to all the forms of literature that he touched. Bharati's was the voice of this newly awakened national consciousness.

He is truly the father of the present era in Tamil, and though it is now more than fifty years since he passed away, his influence is still powerful. And his influence is just, for he is the only Tamil poet of consequence who has striven to bring to the Tamils a sense of national unity. "He has used the Tamils' love of their language to direct them to a love, not merely of Tamilnadu, but the whole of India. He is one of the major landmarks of Tamil literature."[10] It was high time for Tamil to be released from the clutches and stagnation of the petty courts of landlords and landowners and the monastic houses of religious orders and come to "a common-sense outlook on life which could be shared by the common people."[11] Tamil was thus brought into the main current of national life. The best in Bharati did that. Tamil verse regained its vigor and naturalness. The Tamilians were given, for the first time in several centuries, a new epoch of poetry, opened up by a poet who breathed freedom and whose breath carried fire with it. However, he did not spurn the past but demanded that the Tamils should recognize the greatness of their language, and also add their original contribution to it by contact with English and through it with the vast treasures of modern European thought.

Today, thanks to Bharati, Tamil literature is studded with a rich, renascent activity. It has returned to its old secularism and democratic outlook without, however, losing its eclecticism and the wealth of tradition derived from it. Novels, short stories, plays, and a new literary criticism based on the aesthetics of the West have all come into being, and work of a high literary quality is being produced. Tamil literature is very much alive today; it is the voice of over thirty million people; it has a great past to inspire it, a vital present, and a luminous future; and this is due mainly to Subramanya Bharati. This is what makes him the bard of the Tamilians, the sovereign among the prime poets of Tamilnadu, a historian of its heart, a chronicler of its consciousness.

It must be remarked here that Bharati was a Brahmin who was heroic enough to fight against orthodox Brahminism. He even dared to cry down the Hindu *smritis,* as a "trap," since they discriminate between Brahmin and non-Brahmin in law. It is no wonder that he "endeared himself to the Tamils and made them feel that he was one with them and of them."[12] Bharati's prose is direct, elastic, functional, and one stride ahead of the prose of his day. Yet by itself it could not have ensured him an immortality. His passport to immortality is his verse. Passionate outpourings of a heart thirsting for freedom, the simple delight in the eternal graces of childhood and young womanhood; the recognition of some of the permanent and universal values of life; mystical and religious emotions — these are what have made Bharati's lyrics famous all over Tamilnadu. No discerning reader can miss the divine spark in Bharati. Reading a lyric of his one can instantly recognize it as genuine poetry. His *Kuyil-Pattu* (Song of a Cuckoo) is a lovely fantasy, the exercise of a true poet in an idle mood with his passion spent. The best in Bharati is in his lyrics, *Tesiya Kidangal* and *Kannan Pattu,* for he then shows a complete mastery of the technique, especially in the richness of imagination, in lyrical charm and rapture, in melody, and in the outburst of pure emotion and feeling. These lyrics will long survive his patriotic songs. He is a pioneer of the simple and easy diction in prose and poetry and has done more for the Tamils as a shaping and guiding force than, for instance, Tiruvalluvar or Kamban. Deeply rooted in tradition and yet endowed with a modern and cosmopolitan outlook, Bharati remains the bridge through which a stranger may enter the heart of Tamil civilization.

His tradition was closely followed by, among others, Bharati Dasan, Kavimani Desikavinyakam Pillai, and S.D.S. Yogi who all died recently. In many respects, the tradition is still being continued by the new generation of Tamil writers especially in "liberality of outlook, in softness and mellowness of sound, in pliability and adjustability to different purposes."[13] Modern Tamil writers and poets regard Bharati as a guiding post and seek in him the standard by which to measure their creative art. It is surely a fitting tribute to the great poet, who is justly called the father of the modern Tamil renaissance, a patriot, a social reformer, and one of the architects of free India.

CHAPTER 2

A Short Biography

"THERE is nothing more beautiful than a December sky," says Kalidas. A December sky is more than a December sky when it is washed, as it was washed on the occasion of Subramanya Bharati's birth, from horizon to horizon with the refulgent silver of full moon light. Subramanya was born on December 11, 1882, at Ettayapuram. The setting and surroundings in which he was born were a panorama with a beauty all its own. According to the Tamil calendar, he was born under the star "Moolam" in the month Karthigai of the year Chitrabhanu. There is a popular Tamil saying that a male child born under this star will lead a royal life. This seems to have come true of Bharati, who is certainly the prince of modern Tamil poetry.

Ettayapuram was then under a Zamindar (an Indian landowner paying a fixed land tax to the British Government) who preferred to be known as a "Raja." It is now in the Tirunelveli District in Tamilnadu, but during the early British rule in South India it was regarded as one of the more important minor principalities of the then Madras Presidency, and its rulers were well known for their generosity to men of learning. It lies about 300 miles south of Madras, in the belt of India's southernmost district which stretches from the Palni range of the Western Ghats to the southernmost point of the peninsula. The Arabian Sea, Bay of Bengal, and Indian Ocean meet only a few miles from here. It is a land of extraordinary richness and fertility, showing even in the dry season a wealth of foliage that to the visitor seems almost incredible. From June to October (with the average rainfall of over 100 inches) Ettayapuram bursts into a green paradise of astonishing loveliness. Ettayapuram's prodigal variety of natural beauty and splendor can hardly have been without its influence in tuning Bharati's mind to that discerning love of nature which his poetry shows in such abundance. The town's present population is 10,742, and most of its inhabitants are descendants of the earliest Dravidians. The people are friendly and courteous. They greet the visitors by saying "Vanakkam" which means "Goodday" and entertain their guests with music and dance. Almost anyone in the town can guide the visitor to a small hamlet where Bharati was born, for here the people of Tamilnadu have raised a memorial to the poet in the same hamlet. The memorial is the first of its kind in India in recent times. It is certainly not a memorial for a Maharaja or one of the ruling class nor was it raised by the government or the idle rich. It was the spontaneous, willing gift of the millions all over Tamilnadu for a great patriot and poet who lived and died for them. "This memorial was raised in 1948, a few months after the country became free of British rule."[1]

Subramanya Bharati's father, Chinnaswami Iyer, came to Ettayapuram in search of a living from the nearby village of Sivalaperi in 1875. He was a noble Brahmin, well versed in Tamil, English, mathematics, and logic. Besides, he was greatly interested in Western technology. Even in those days he was able to open any machine part by part and reassemble the whole mechanism accurately. Because he combined the old and the new so well, he gained a prominent position in the Ettayapuram court. The Raja was also impressed by Chinnaswami's poetry and many a time he played the role of his court poet. But Chinnaswami's fertile mind thought up many schemes, and in 1880 he managed to install the first cotton ginning mill at Ettayapuram, one of the few early pioneering technological ventures in South India. He was not only endowed with the gift of native intelligence and natural curiosity, but also with a handsome appearance. While he had the usual Dravidian dark complexion, his penetrating keen eyes were admired by all. He was generally respected by his peers because of his religious piety and mystic temperament. He kept the company of Brahmins, from whom he acquired a great deal of Vedic knowledge and was a frequent visitor to the seashore temple of Subramanya at Tituchandur.

Chinnaswami Iyer married his first cousin Lakshmi, who was known to be graceful and of a kindly disposition. She was also a deeply religious woman. Though she acquired no formal education, different forms of religious duties and a deep consciousness of belief and right doing were an integral part of her. The two led a happy and contented married life. Their first son was named Subramanya after the Lord of Tituchandur. It was later fondly abbreviated to Subbiah. The birth of the first child in Chinnaswami's house caused much domestic happiness and the child became the darling of the family. Subbiah's family circle at Ettayapuram was fairly large. His maternal grandparents, his cousins, and his young uncle also lived in the same town. His grandfather, Ramaswamy Iyer, was an indulgent friend to the young Subbiah. Young Subbiah often used to go out of the city limits with his grandfather, where they would pass the day singing religious lyrics that he loved, interspersed with lighter frolics. The old man's knowledge of Tamil culture and religious discipline was considerable, and Subbiah learned from Ramaswamy Iyer many stories from the *Ramayana, Kural,* and other ancient Tamil mythologies. What Bharati learned by gentle communion in childhood became an inspiration for him in his later years; this knowledge he profitably used in his literary creations, particularly in his mystic poems.

When Bharati was five years old this earliest and happy home life of his was suddenly broken up by his mother's death. It was an irreparable loss the shock of which he never got over. He felt the absence of his mother greatly and even late in his life he would suffer from pangs of regret on hearing the word "mother" casually uttered by anyone in his presence.

Lakshmi's father came to Subbiah's rescue and took a personal interest in the boy's education. The mother's place was taken by Lakshmi's younger sister Sita who married his father. During his father's second marriage, Subbiah was invested with the sacred thread ceremony. His stepmother proved very kind to the young poet who was fast developing into a precocious child. Even at that age, Bharati would attract the attention of people around him by his witty talk. A childhood associate of his recalls vividly Bharati's early days. He used to sing verses extempore even at this age and astound poetical elders who tested him with all kinds of tricks of versification. The young boy's powers of poesy pleased every one — except perhaps his father, who had his own ideas of making him learn the exact sciences and mathematics so as to enable him to succeed in life. The father did not encourage Subbiah's interest in Tamil poetry, and so the young boy used to play truant and hide himself in the corner of a local temple to enjoy Tamil classics unmolested.

Subbiah truly detested regular schooling. Along with his young uncle Sambasivam, he would undertake boyish exploits and spend hours without sparing a single thought for his studies. Whenever Chinnaswami Iyer settled down seriously to teach the errant boy, the latter would be lost in day dreams or would be composing impromptu verses in Tamil. Nor could the teachers in his school ensure his attention to studies. What was to be done with a student who jumped at any word uttered by the teacher and started a series of rhymes!

Bharati's loneliness was accentuated by his father's sternness. Indeed, several times, his stepmother seems to have eased many a tricky moment between the stern father and the son. He was not allowed to have friends of his age group. The father, angered by his son's intractability, thought that he was punishing him in this way! There is an aching reference to this phase in Bharati's auto-biography.

Hitherto he had given but little thought to turning his loneliness into a seeking of inner worlds; but an elderly Tamil scholar of the town used to read to him occasionally Kamban's *Ramayana,* Tiruvalluvar's *Kural* and the poems of Thayumanavar. This tutelage sufficiently developed his first and undying love for the angel Poesy which he has thus expressed:

> As two birds in love
>   Happy in a forest,
> Or gods and goddesses
>   In an amorous swoon,
> Not flawed by mundane joys
>   But joined in ecstasy,
> I spent some divine days
>   With that honey-sweet Being.

His grandfather, Ramaswami Iyer, was, however, sympathetic to this intoxication and taught him some classical Tamil poetry. His father continued to frown upon Bharati's Tamil studies because he wanted the boy to come up in the world, which meant a mastery of English. Worried about his son's future, he decided to send Subbiah to Tirunelveli for his high school education.

I   *Education: Tirunelveli*

At Tirunelveli, Bharati missed most the company of his sympathetic grandfather and affectionate stepmother. He had uncles in Tirunelveli to look after him, but they could not provide the warmth of understanding that the lonely poet needed. He spent three mechanical years going through the high school grind in the Hindu College. In later years he looked upon this period as the darkest patch in his life. He was aflame with the love of Tamil literature but he had to forget all about it and study English and "foreign" sciences. He writes bitterly:

> My father ordered me to Nellai
>> To acquire the "foreign" knowledge.
> As if feeding a lion cub
>> With grass.

However life for him during these three years moved on like the most regular of verbs — "reading," "playing," producing verses on the spur of the moment. Aristotle said that "to be happy means to be self sufficient." Subbiah was "self sufficient" and therefore "happy." His genius for composing impromptu verses made him the most sought after boy in the whole school. He made humorous lines caricaturing the teachers in the most comic poses. They were phrased in simple colloquial Tamil and in easy tunes, and the boys sang them aloud. The Tamil teacher Sivarama Pillai known for his stiff adherence to pedantic language became a target. Pillai was aware of all laughter at his expense, for the boys made no attempt to hide it, and he bided his time.

Once, Sivarama Pillai was angered by some intransigence on Bharati's part. Seeing that he was sitting on the topmost bench of the gallery whispering in the middle of his period, the teacher called out, "Can you tell me, C. Subramanya, what I have been telling the class?" Taken by surprise, Bharati stood up tongue-tied. The teacher twitted:

> "You are said to pour verses like the dark cloud above
> Like the clouds you are hovering above
> Why do you not pour answers like
> Kala Megham [the dark cloud] to my questions?"

The class sat tense with expectation. What would Subbiah say? Stung to the quick Bharati retorted:

> "The learned Pandit has overlooked
> One simple but well-known fact.
> The clouds pour rain at their will and pleasure
> Not because of a ruling by some Pandit."

A titter ran through the class. Bharati had won. Sivarama Pillai flushed and muttered, "You have a ready wit."

Such triumphs in impromptu versification daily swelled the ranks of his friends. Life was to him then a panorama with distinctive landmarks; this distinction manifested itself most succinctly in keeping his friends in good spirits with his humorous, gay, and stinging repartees. While lying lazily on the sandy banks of the Tamraparni he would recite light verses about those who he thought were stick-in-the-mud elders. The boys whistled, clapped, and burst into roars of laughter.

But such triumphs did little to quiet the worries of his father. Added to his cares, Subbiah also failed to get through the matriculation examination. This dashed Chinnaswami Iyer's dreams of seeing his son becoming an influential official or a learned professor. It was a cruel misfortune for his father who had had rosy dreams of his son's future. Whether Bharati suffered inwardly we do not know. He certainly put on a cheerful front and returned to Ettayapuram visibly relieved. He tells us in his autobiography that he was thus saved from being completely spoiled by the "foreign" education.

At Ettayapuram, he was welcomed by the Raja who gave him a job. Subbiah soon became his favorite, partly because he was Chinnaswami's son and partly because Bharati himself possessed a maturity of mind that was far in advance of his age. But a favorite has no friend, it is said; and Subbiah certainly managed to gather a few enemies at the Raja's court, because he was very outspoken, sometimes even to the point of rudeness. One member of this hostile group tried to humiliate him publicly by referring to his failure in the Hindu College in rather demeaning terms. Subbiah's anger flared up. Honor bound, he challenged the accuser to an open contest of wits. The Raja was present when the great debate took place. The subject was "education." After a learned Pandit had opened the debate on behalf of the courtier, Subbiah got up and made a brilliant speech full of humor and eloquence. The arguments were perfectly structured, and the audience including the Raja was speechless with amazement. An elderly Pandit respected widely for his learning rose to praise Subbiah for his wise words and conferred on him the title of Bharati (one of the names of the Hindu Goddess Saraswati). "From that historic moment in 1893, Subbiah became Bharati and he is still fondly referred to by this name by millions of his fans all over the world."[2]

This made Bharati locally well known too. Service with the Raja gave him all the leisure he needed for studying Tamil literature and practising poetry. His father watched with sadness, all his dreams fading away.

II *Marriage*

In June, 1897, Bharati was married at the age of fifteen. The traditional marriage ceremonies of those days went on for five days. They were more for the enjoyment of the community, than for the bride and the bridegroom. There were dance recitals, concerts, shows, and clarinet performances. The budding poet took active interest in all these cultural activities. The seven-year-old bride Chellamma, daughter of Chellappa Iyer of Kadayam, was sweet and shy. She had a small oval face and soft brown eyes like those of a fawn. She darted bashful glances at her youthful husband from under her fluttering eyelashes while he relished with gusto the music and the dance. To his young bride, blushing with shyness, Bharati addressed this poem:

> Mirror of life, Oh, priceless gem!
> Dear princess, like a swan you move.
> The arrow of love has struck my heart.
> I cannot eat, I cannot sleep.

Chellamma trembled at this strange and fiery wooing. Tradition ruled that the bridegroom should not even talk to the bride, let alone address verses to her so openly. The company burst into derisive laughter and the bride, driven to tears, shrank within herself with shame. She hardly heeded her father, who was bursting with pride, when he told her she had married a genius. At the end of the festivities, Bharati had sung a whole poem on the celebrations, praising the tastefully decorated pavilion, the entertainments, and the lavish hospitality of the host.

Bharati saw her confusion and laughed. It sounded so like the ripples of a musical scale that little Chellamma was thrilled by it. "Never mind, beloved, I'll teach you the meaning of true love," he said. This bewildered the young bride even more. But when the time came for parting before joining him at his home, she shed tears. He had been such good company during the long boring hours of ceremonial.

Recalling the event later, Bharati's wife said, "My husband would go on singing love songs unabashedly to the delight of all present. But I felt very shamefaced at not having been blessed with a normal husband for my lifemate."

The poet probably did not feel all that he sang at the time of his marriage. He was, after all, too young. To a boy of those days, child marriage was a natural event and he had acceded to his father's plans without a murmur. But in later life he felt that his early marriage had shackled him rather too soon with heavy responsibilities and prevented him from completely dedicating himself to his first love — poetry. In his autobiography he writes: "Ere my understanding grew I had twin masters: Love and Duty."

This clash between love and duty — love to write creatively and duty to provide for the needs of the family — broke upon him soon enough. The idyllic Ettayapuram life was rudely shattered when Chinnaswamy Iyer died in 1898. Bharati says that his father was too much influenced by what was happening in the west and foolishly sank all his wealth in business, dreaming of making a fortune. More likely his father regarded himself as an idealist attempting to become the first industrial entrepreneur in the Tirunelveli district. Financial ruin closed upon him when his printing press and ginning mill at Ettayapuram ground to a dead loss. He was rudely shocked by other monetary difficulties that came upon him in the wake of this disaster. Heartbroken and penniless, he passed away, leaving his family destitute. Ill equipped, barely twenty and saddled with a wife, the young poet found that he had no means of earning a livelihood.

III   *Study at Benares*

His father's sister Kuppammal and her husband Krishna Sivan lived at Benares. They had always loved Bharati and now, seeing his plight, invited him to study at this ancient seat of learning. He bade a quick farewell to his aging grandparents, promised Chellamma he would be back soon, and left Ettayapuram. His uncle reasoned that once Bharati gained an academic degree, he could take up a regular job and start keeping house with Chellamma in reasonable comfort. Bharati, too, by this time, felt a pang at his past attitude to formal education. He realized that he should have worked hard at his studies while at Tirunelveli. Without a formal education it was difficult to go out into the world in search of a career. But he was no mere dreamer and was capable of quick purposive action. He soon joined the Central Hindu College, Benares, and passed the entrance examination in A grade; and this was done in spite of the fact that he had to study two entirely new languages — Sanskrit and Hindi.

Benares had so impressed Bharati that he started dressing in the north Indian fashion, cutting his hair, growing a moustache, and wearing an enormous turban. The city's long, narrow, zigzag streets, the endless procession of devotees, and incessant chant of *mantras* on the banks of the colorful Ganga made "an indelible impression on the poet."[3] He was struck by the contrast between man's pettiness and nature's infinite majesty. Here, there was no dearth of scholars and thinkers. Bharati spent a great deal of his time discussing with them the eternal problems of life. Unlike most of them he was appalled by the ignorance of his countrymen and their quiet acceptance of poverty and disease as part of life. What pained him even more was the complete indifference and lack of interest in those who should stand up for their own rights. Indeed, the picture of his own wife doomed to obscurity behind soot-covered kitchen walls incensed him. In one of his letters to her from Benares he urged her to learn to read so that she could understand better the life around her.

The shadow of his own penury cast a gloom over him even then. He was aware of his heavy responsibility and after passing his entrance examination, took a poorly paid teaching job. These were hard days for him. His friend in Benares, S. Narayana Iyengar, writes about those days thus:

Subbiah was in dire poverty. I was surprised to see his interest in current politics was nil. . . . Whenever he had leisure he would recite Shelley's poetry to us and explain the nuances of the English poet. He had little training in Sanskrit. But he had immense pleasure in listening to expositions of Sanskrit poetry.

If Bharati showed little interest in politics, he was intensely alive to the ills that infested Indian society. Tradition could not hold him in its grip. He became almost obsessed with the idea of equality of the sexes and showed interest in women's education. Thus, during the Benares interlude, he developed two important interests. The first was love for English poetry. Often with a book of English poems in hand he would wander along the banks of the Ganga, dreaming and meditating. This widened the traditional concept of poetry with which he had been hitherto familiar. At once Bharati's poetry was released from the straightjacket of punditry and grew glowing wings. Of equal importance was Bharati's interest in the status of women which gave him a "general taste of rebellion" and led him directly to the struggle for Indian Independence. He learned to question things, especially "India's social structure or the basis of British rule."[4]

IV *Back to Ettayapuram*

In 1902 the Raja after attending Edward VII's *durbar* at Delhi visited Benares. Some of the courtiers who saw Bharati suffering privations requested the Raja to take Bharati into his service. The Raja agreed, and Bharati returned to Ettayapuram.

During the next two years Bharati led an easy life reading the papers to the Raja and acting as a sort of a poet companion to him. Being by nature a fiercely independent person, Bharati was indeed irked by the emptiness of court life and the conditions of inequality between persons. Besides, he was disgusted by the Raja's preference for erotic poetry and vulgar scandals. Again, the Raja taught him the odious habit of opium taking which completely undermined his health and was to prove ruinous in his later days when he resorted to it to alleviate the pangs of hunger. There was, however, a brighter side to his Ettayapuram stay. Steadily, Bharati used all his hours of leisure to study great literature — particularly that of the ancient Tamils. Many years later he wrote an autobiographical fragment titled, *Chinna Sankaran Kathai.* In this there is a hilarious and accurate picture of his Ettayapuram days and of the personality of the Raja who befriended him. After two years of this "foxy existence," Bharati decided to escape from the place and earn his livelihood through honest albeit hard work. His leaving Ettayapuram was also precipitated by a misunderstanding between the Raja and himself over some unguarded remarks of Bharati that seemed to disparage royalty. With characteristic nonchalance Bharati wrote a satirical poem on the Raja as a parting shot and left the place of his birth.

From Ettayapuram Bharati went to the nearby town of Madurai. He was eager to explore things. The gates to freedom now stood wide open for him. Through the help of his friend M. Gopala Krishna Iyer, he got a job as a teacher of Tamil in Setupati High School on the first of August 1904.

It was only in the previous month that a poem of his entitled "Solitude" had been published for the first time in the Tamil magazine *Vivekabhanu* of Madurai. It has Wordsworthian echoes, although written in the hard, tongue-twisting style of the old time pundits. But Bharati was already divesting himself of these traditional appurtenances. He must have been a successful teacher because of his wide mastery of Tamil literature. A student of his in those days refers to the bright-eyed Bharati as a slender figure of medium height. His bronze face was encased in a lovely pale colored turban, partly covering the broad forehead on which shone a deep red mark. He had a perfectly well-proportioned nose, and fine eyes spitting fire. A moustache set off his lips which were soft like a woman's. Over his shirt he wore a long alpaca coat meant to be buttoned up to the neck. He wore his *dhoti* in the traditional style, wound round his legs and tucked between his thighs. He was frail but vibrant with energy. "Even then one felt the special magnetism of his eyes. But we never realized his greatness." The temporary job came to an end on November 10, 1904, when G. Subramania Iyer, editor of the Tamil daily *Swadesmitran,* offered him a job as an assistant editor at Madras. From then onwards there was no looking back for Bharati. The voice of freedom inside the poet urged him to go on with what seemed to him his purpose in life. He began his sway over the mind of the Tamil people.

V *Assistant Editor*

We next find Bharati in a dingy back room of a large boxlike house in George Town, Madras. The house had rooms opening into the courtyard and many families lived in them huddled together, side by side. The air was hot and stuffy with the breath of so many in so small a space. At night the children wailed, an asthmatic tenant coughed incessantly, and the water dripped from the only pipe in the courtyard. If in spite of all this one dozed off, it was not for long because of the mosquitoes. Used to Chinnaswamy's large house in Ettayapuram, Chellamma felt cramped and unhappy. Her little Thangam, a one-year-old, was constantly ill with colds and coughs. It was the beginning of long years of hardship for her.

Bharati's major work in the office was to translate into Tamil news appearing in English dailies. This is not as easy as it sounds. Translating modern English into Tamil that was not yet free of punditry called for courage and resourcefulness. But Bharati could be at once unconventional and intelligible. Again, the prevailing temper of national politics demanded superhuman self-restraint on the part of the translator. He had to be accurate and fair. This was the "workshop" period for Bharati. His genius gave the Tamils a natural and elastic written language for their new literature. The speed with which he translated the English news into simple, elegant, readable Tamil was extraordinary. G. Subramania Iyer marveled at his skill. He wrote rapidly; words seemed to flow out of him as water from a fount. With fluent ease, he discussed in his newspaper social problems in Japan, political ferment in Russia, or racial conflict in Africa. As for Indian affairs, he saw everything with a fresh eye. Whether it was literature, music, fresh interpretation of Vedic thoughts, social questions of the day, the speeches of Swami Vivekananda or Sri Aurobindo or the Presidential addresses at the sessions of the Indian National Congress he treated them in a light and lively manner. By dint of sheer hard work, young Bharati became a model for Tamil journalists. No wonder Subramania Iyer became very fond of Bharati. But he was also clever in getting the maximum amount of work from him. V. Ramaswamy, an associate of Bharati in Pondicherry, reports in his biography of the poet these words of Bharati himself:

"I would be sitting in my office chair in the evening, thinking about going home. I would be in need of some money, so I would wonder whether to ask Iyer for it or not. Suddenly a servant would come in with a tumbler of coffee and say that it was sent by Subramania Iyer. I would be wafted to the seventh heaven by this demonstration of love. At this moment, Iyer would appear. I would forget about asking him for money. 'Bharati, have you seen the moving speech on India delivered in England by Sir Henry Cotton?' 'Yes, I have; he has spoken very well,' I would reply. 'Oughtn't we to publish it tomorrow in our paper?' he would ask. 'Certainly we ought.' 'Who except you can translate it into Tamil without losing the surge of feeling?' Iyer would tell me. I would stand with bowed head. 'There is no need for you to translate it in the office. Take it home and bring the translation tomorrow morning. That would be enough. You could translate it in a jiffy. It wouldn't take you above half an hour.' "[5]

Of course Bharati would comply with the request, for he was grateful to Iyer for giving him his real start in life. He would often relate Iyer's words: "Bharati, you write wonderful Tamil. One could give a million rupees for every word. Your *are* Kalidas. But I am no king Bhoj!"

After a few months of getting accustomed to the new job, Bharati's poetic voice began to be articulate again. The first poem of his to appear in *Swadesmitran* was "Hail Bengal" on September 15, 1905. Since the paper was moderate in its tone and policy, Bharati was not allowed to do editorials or publish his own articles. But along with the hack work, Bharati also began to exert himself in the cause of social reform. His frank, open ways and humorous conversation won him many friends. He became the life and soul of a group that was known as the Radical Reform Club. Its members came from all castes. Their common vow was the uplift of Indian society. "Some of the prominent members of this group were S. Doraiswami Iyer, an advocate who is still alive but living in voluntary seclusion; V. Chakkarai Chetty, who later became a renowned labor leader; C.S. Raghunatha Rao, a journalist; a teacher by name Paul; Jayaram

Naidu, a doctor of medicine; Surendranath Arya, a pugnacious young political worker; Subramania Siva, a national worker and V.O. Chidambaram Pillai, an astute politician. The group was encouraged by Ramasesha Iyer, proprietor of Ganesh and Company, well known publishers of Madras."[6] In their zeal to demolish the barriers of caste the group members made no distinction among themselves. The lower caste members cooked and all of them ate with relish. Bharati, especially, loved good food, and his friends would tease him. "What happens to all the food you eat at our expense, Bharati? You look so thin that a strong sea breeze could knock you down," said S. Doraiswami. "His strength is that of his mind," said V.O. Chidambaram Pillai. "His words are strong. They go to the head like ripe toddy," said Chakkarai Chetty.

The circle came to be the talk of Madras city. Other Brahmins were shocked that men like Bharati and Doraiswami should eat in the company of those who were not Brahmins. Some of them had reasons to be displeased. Bharati had openly criticized the meek manner in which the prominent citizens of Madras submitted to social tyranny.

Poor Chellamma was the butt of many cruel slings from her neighbors and friends, and she moaned her lot. It was both a pleasure and a torture to live with Bharati. She adored his sensitiveness and tender love but could not bear his strange moods, his passion for things that seemed to her meaningless, and his urgent protestations to give up even life rather than submit to certain social ills.

These young friends from all walks of life soon started an English weekly called *Radical Social Reform*. Often they met at the Marina sea beach in Madras. The roar of the sea drowned their voices raised in arguing social issues of the day. Every social problem was thrashed out on the sands of the Bay of Bengal. Bharati sang his songs. With the salt blowing on his face, the young poet composed vivid verses on the sea, the sun, the clouds, and the sand. His audience listened, transported to a world of imagery. The following poem is an example of his description of the sun:

> O Sun, what hast thou done to darkness?
> Didst thou drive it away, kill it or devour it?
> Hast thou enfolded it in your hard embrace and
> Kissed it, enveloping it with your rays?
> Is darkness your foe?
> Is darkness your food?

Or has it become your beloved?
Has she swooned away in gloom at your absence
from her the whole of the night?
Seeing you, she has merged herself with
you, filling herself with your light.
Are you both children of the same mother?
Has your mother bidden you both appear,
One following the other, to protect life on earth?
Have you no death? Are you immortal?
I adore thee
O Sun, I worship thee.

Deeply affected by the impact of the new age and the newly won gift of simple prose, Bharati shed the difficult classical style. His poetry took on a new quality of excellence. It began to scintillate with joy, passion, and fervor but was couched in words that reached the heart of everyone. "People gathered on the beach when he sang. His audience listened in spellbound silence."[7]

The poet's mind, thrown open to new sensations, was about to take flight on its wings, when it received a fresh impetus. Bharati had gone to the meeting of the Indian National Congress at Benares in 1905 which was presided over by Gopal Krishna Gokhale. Gokhale was a known moderate and at this session he had to face the extremists led by the trio, Bepin Chandra Pal, Lajpat Rai, and Lokmanya Tilak. It was Tilak's passion and love of the motherland that swept Bharati off his feet, and he began to share Tilak's extremist views. His articles and views of the period show that in his view Tilak's extremist policy was the only hope of early freedom for India. He gave vent to his feelings in his famous lines "Long live Tilak's name / Fall, let fall the tyrant's rule."

VI   *Meeting with Sister Nivedita*

With the partitioning of Bengal by Lord Curzon, Bharati became increasingly conversant with what was happening to India's political life, because his job at *Swadesmitran* made him study current political events from all angles. He also attended the next session of the Congress at Calcutta which was presided over by Dadabhai Naoroji. While in Calcutta, the most significant event of Bharati's life occurred, the impact of which made a deep and lasting impression on the poet's mind. It was there that he met Sister Nivedita, an English woman by birth and the first nun of the Ramakrishna Order. Sister Nivedita was a disciple of Swami Vivekananda and a great social worker who encouraged women's education in Bengal with a missionary zeal.

At first glance the poet recognized in her traces of divinity. He made obeisance to her and stood with great reverence. Then she spoke to him: "My son, remove all your mental reservations. Forget uncivilized differentiations such as caste, creed and birth. Enthrone love in your heart. You will become a divine being enshrined in the pages of history." Is it possible that Sister Nivedita saw in Bharati's eyes something unusual, the gleam of future greatness? But let us read what Bharati himself has to say about this meeting:

"Do you know, Doraiswami, I had a feeling of being lifted out of myself. The lustre around her was like that of the very sun's golden light. She cried, 'Mother India is in handcuffs and is suffering as a slave. Will you have the courage to set her free? Look, see if you have the nerve to stab into white breasts like mine.' So saying she bared her chest to me. Can you believe, she is English."

Doraiswami murmured, "Impossible."

"It is true. It happened and the picture of Nivedita is carved in my mind never to be erased. The scales have fallen from my eyes. I know now what I must live for. There was another matter about which she made me blush. The way I treat my wife — the way all of us treat our women," he stammered as he spoke.

"Did she preach equality of status?" asked Doraiswami who was a lawyer.

"No. No. It was more than that. She urged that we treat them as part of ourselves which is exactly what our scriptures tell us to do. Does it not remind you of how Siva held Parvati on his left and made her one with him? So did Brahma hold Saraswati on his tongue and Lakshmi clung to Vishnu's broad chest."

Doraiswami marvelled at his friend. He seemed as one possessed; his eyes wore a far off look and passion shook his body. His eyelids dropped and he sank into a dream. Later Bharati extolled Mother India in a fitting poem which is in the shape of questions and answers:

> Whose was the bow, that ages back,
> Worked a debacle on Lanka's giants?
> That was the bow of our Aryan queen,
> Our furious mother, Bharata Devi.
>
> Whose was the world, that proclaimed,
> That all our miseries could be overcome,

If only firmness gets implanted in the world of our mind?
That was the word of our Aryan queen.

Bharati had accepted Nivedita as his *Guru*. She had fused into him
a blinding spiritual revelation and social teachings in the course of a
single interview. While parting, Sister Nivedita gave a dried leaf to
Bharati as a memento. She had brought it from her Himalayan
journey. And Bharati revered it till the end of his days, guarding it
with jealous care. Even during his poverty-stricken days, he refused
to part with it, though he was offered enormous sums in exchange,
for it. The holy leaf was lost after his death; what still lives as a
memorial is Bharati's invocation:

Nivedita, Mother
Thou Temple consecrated to Love
Thou, Sun dispelling my Soul's darkness
Thou Rain to the parched land of our times
Thou, helper of the helpless and lost
Thou, offering to Grace
Thou divine spark of Truth,
My salutations to Thee!

After his meeting with Nivedita, Bharati was restless and dis-
satisfied with his lot. G. Subramania Iyer now appeared to him to be
too cautious, too prudent. Often he warned the poet and admonished
him for his rashness.

"You must be more careful in your language. Remember, the
country is not yet ripe to receive your fiery message. Also the
foreigner is sitting pretty," he said in quiet tones. Bharati felt
frustrated. He wanted more freedom to pour out his impassioned
words to his countrymen. He burned with the fervor of freedom. His
extreme political views made it necessary for him to leave the
Swadesmitran since he now wanted a paper that would give him the
freedom to "write" and to "publish."

The Radical Reform Club now became the meeting place for all
progressive thinkers as well as men of action. "Swadesi" was their
slogan. "We shall be ruled by Indians, speak or write Indian
languages, wear Indian clothes and produce all that we need
ourselves," they vowed. It was in this spirit that the Mandayam
brothers, Tirumalachari and Srinivasachari — two extremist
followers of Tilak — turned to Bharati saying "Why not start a
Tamil weekly of our own? How can we hope to spread the spirit of

nationalism throughout the land unless we have the means to reach the people?''

The poet laughed. "Nothing would be better. The people should be told how our life, our very breath, is being stifled. It is time to awaken their minds to the true state of our country and sow the seeds of discontent.''

"Will you undertake to edit the paper if we start one?" asked Srinivasachari.

"Gladly," replied Bharati. Then his face fell. "G. Subramania Iyer restricts my expression. He will not allow me to speak out. Will you give me the freedom to say what I want?

"Readily."

The poet's face lit up with joy. "I have long been yearning for such a chance. The spirit of patriotism is dead in our land. I want to reawaken it and guide the people towards concrete goals. You will not regret having chosen me.''

VII   *Editor of India*

Tirumalachari's Tamil weekly was known as *India*. Born in April, 1906, *India* soon came to be known as the most daring of nationalistic papers. Not caring in the least whether he offended the British Government in India, Bharati boldly exposed the sickness in the land. He roundly accused the British of selfishness, loudly called to the people to stir themselves, and openly poked fun at those prominent citizens whose interest in public welfare was of the milk-and-water type. Such men, he said, were afraid of offending the English. They played for safety, preferring mere promises to action. For the first time, in the history of Tamil journalism, a demand for full independence of India was made openly and squarely by Bharati. People were so moved by Bharati's writing that they began to burn English goods in public places. It was action at last.

He also started tirelessly to address public meetings and mesmerize vast audiences in Madras with his melodious voice singing patriotic songs, one of which, freely translated, runs as follows:

> When will subside this thirst for liberty;
> When will perish our love for servitude?
> Oh! when will snap our mother's manacles?
> And when will our troubles cease and become null?
> Oh! thou, that came once for the Bharat's war,
> Thou, Protector of Aryans' lives!

Is it not thy mercy to assist us with victory?
Is it proper Thy devotees still suffer?
Are famines and epidemics [reserved] for Thy true servants?
To whom else is all greatness in this world?
Canst Thou give up those who have
                                        taken shelter under Thee.
And can the Mother cast her child away?
Is it not Thy duty to say "Fear not,"
Oh! Arya, Hast Thou forgotten thy virtue!
Oh! Thou, Destroyer of the evil Rakshasas [demon]
Oh! Gem of Warriors, Oh! Best of Aryans!

This was the period when, carried away by the thought of freedom, Bharati bloomed into a true poet. Gone was the stylized mode of classical poetry. Gone were the stilted verses with words known only to scholars, and difficult turns of grammar. Bharati now wrote for the common man. His poems were free, easy, and flowing, going straight to the hearts of simple people. The impact was tremendous. Bharati set them to music using the tunes of the popular Nandanar musical. People who went to hear him on the Marina beach carried the songs into the heart of the city. They caught on like fire and soon the songs were on everyone's lips.

He dedicated two of his first verse collections to Sister Nivedita. The dedication of *Swadesa Gitangal* reads: "I place this slim volume at the Teacher's feet who showed me the vision of Mother Bharat [India] and instilled in me patriotism, even as Sri Krishna revealed to Arjuna His Viswarupa and taught him the true nature of the Self." A year later, in 1909, he dedicated *Janma Bhoomi* also to Sister Nivedita: "I dedicate this book to Srimati Nivedita Devi, the dharmaputri of Bhagwan Vivekananda, who without words, in a split second, taught me the nature of true service to the Mother and the greatness of sacrifice."

Bharati was now clearly identified with the extremist group in Congress. After his meetings with Tilak, Sri Aurobindo, and Lala Lajpat Rai, Bharati's articles and poems became more fiery and violent. *India* became a virulent critic of the Raj and had by now earned a reputation as a firebrand. The anxious British Government promptly arrested the publisher of *India*. It needed no prophet to say that Bharati, too, might be arrested. On the advice of his friends and well-wishers, he went into voluntary exile at Pondicherry, which was then a part of French India. He thus became the "first Indian politician to take refuge in Pondicherry."[8]

VIII   *Pondicherry*

Within two days of his arrival, the British Indian police traced Bharati. Thereafter they gave him no rest. Since the poet was in French territory the police could do nothing, because they had no authority to arrest him. But their veiled threats put Bharati in an agony of despair. They started harassing him with little pin pricks and tried hard to lure him to British India so that they might arrest him. Despite such provocations Bharati stayed in Pondicherry with the help of a number of his admirers who even went to the extent of pawning their family jewelry and possessions to help the poet.

It was now becoming increasingly difficult to publish *India* in Madras. After Bharati's flight, the police became more vigilant and started provoking the owners of *India*. The Mandayam brothers decided to follow Bharati to Pondicherry. They managed to convey the printing machines in secret and install them in a rented house in Rue Dupleix. The poet greeted this move with joy. Gone was his despondency. He set to work on his paper once again. *India* took a fresh lease of life and breathed the spirit of Bharati. It became so prosperous that soon the Mandayam brothers decided to publish their daily *Vijaya* also from Pondicherry. The English weekly *Bala Bharata* was also started much to the chagrin of the British Government. Both these publications were also being edited by Bharati.

Bharati's writings embraced a wide range of subjects besides politics. He wrote with awareness of social and political problems in other lands. He wrote of French literature and Japanese Haiku poetry. He quoted English classics. Of the ills of Indian life and superstition he had not a little to say. One of his favorite topics was the treatment of women.

Art and literature, trade and commerce — all found place in journals and newspapers edited by Bharati. His was also one of the first papers in an Indian language to publish cartoons. It had its own arrangement with Reuters. His magazines and papers appealed widely to the people and every copy sold was read by dozens. This prosperity and widespread popularity roused the British Indian government to take punitive action, and they banned all Bharati's newspapers and magazines in British India. This was a serious blow because all Bharati's subscribers were from British India. The publications struggled hard for a time, but finally died one after the other in March, 1910, and the Mandayam brothers closed down the press. By the end of 1910 Bharati was left to face the greatest challenge to his genius — enforced idleness.

Bharati bore this blow with courage. Though outwardly he laughed and sang, inwardly he sagged. Just when he had touched the nadir of depression, a new force reached Pondicherry and saved Bharati from utter collapse. This was Sri Aurobindo who came to Pondicherry in April, 1910. Another person who joined them a few months later was V.V.S. Iyer. Both Sri Aurobindo and Iyer were refugees fleeing from the wrath of the British Indian government. Though honorably acquitted, Sri Aurobindo was charged with having been a party to the violent bomb incidents in Bengal. Iyer belonged to a progressive group of Indians in London one of whom was thought to have murdered a British official. With Bharati and Srinivasachari Mandayam they formed a foursome and discoursed on a wide range of subjects. Bharati, Iyer and Sri Aurobindo were steeped in the literatures of India and the West. Both Sri Aurobindo and Bharati were poets, and Iyer was a well-known short-story writer. Srinivasachari was a sympathetic listener.

Engrossed in philosophical arguments, Bharati forgot sleep and food. These discussions set the tone for the poet's translation of Patanjali's sutras. It was good that Bharati was thus touched with this creative urge. His daily life was riddled with poverty and suffering, and often it appeared they might crush him forever. All the munificence of his friends, all the resourcefulness of his patrons, all the ministrations of his admirers could not save the poet from the slings and arrows of fate. His wife, too, betrayed the strain by often flying into a temper. Often he would soothe her with a song:

> Thou to me the lute of gold,
> And I to thee the finger bold:
> Necklace shining thou to me,
> Newset diamond I to thee:
> O mighty queen with splendour rife,
> O Krishna, Love:
> O well of life,
> Thine eyes do shed their light on all
> Wherever I turn, their beams do fall.[9]

But there was a limit to Chellamma's patience. They had many a wordy war. On such occasions he would silently leave the house. His favorite refuge was the nearby village of Muthyalpet where he had made friends with a weaver, Krishnaswamy Chettiar. He loved to wander in solitude in Krishnaswamy's grove. On one such visit, the poet felt at one with Nature at the sight of the leaves and the flowers, the sound of the distant sea, and the twitter of the birds. He shouted aloud in an ecstasy of joy as he found an echo of the scene in his heart. Sitting on a stone he murmured the musical scales, then stared at the tree and the sky. He got up and stamped upon the bare earth waving his hands about. The throb and anguish, the torture and pain nearly broke the poet. As if in a sweep came the first couplets of his great poem, *Kuvil Pattu* (Song of the Cuckoo), a long love poem full of pathos and tenderness. At the end of the song, the exhausted Bharati fell to the ground unconscious. The shadows of the green trees enveloped him in a loving embrace.

From that year (1912) Bharati wrote incessantly, both poetry and prose, producing hundreds of poems, scores of essays, little stories, animal tales in the manner of the *Panchatantra*, and humorous skits. He went back to the springs of Indian culture. He created visions of rain, sea, grove and garden. He wrote of "Mother" (Supreme Goddess) and the gods of heaven. He had once translated the *Bhagavad Gita*. The poetry of the Vedic seers invested his creations with visionary glow. The Sanskrit classics infused a new strength to his poetic voice. The Tamil *Prabandhas* inculcated a serene faith in God. He wrote as one possessed. He wrote a preface to his translation of the *Bhagavad Gita* which became more famous than the translation. All his major works, the Kannan series, *Kannan Pattu, Kuvil Pattu,* and *Panchali Sapatham* were written in this period. He also put his hand to a humorous novel *Chinna Sankaran Kathai* which was really an autobiographical sketch. Though much of what he created during the Pondicherry years is lost forever, his three great poems and a good deal of thought-provoking journalism remain.

But how long can a person be employed in creative writing that is not productive financially? The need to make ends meet was daily growing more desperate, and by 1915 Bharati had reached the depths of depression. If his family was still able to live, it was because of a regular monthly pension of thirty rupees from his old paper *Swadesmitran*. Fragments of his 1915 diary have come down to us, and they speak volumes about the poverty, the undiminished idealism, the essential mental strength, and the undisturbed faith that kept house together within this storm-tossed person. Never a strong man physically, at this period of life he was ailing for weeks on end. The entries are a veritable monologue in the Supreme Goddess' presence. During the terrible days of poverty, Bharati never prayed or asked for worldly riches. Even for his wife, he wanted everything except riches.

IX *Kadayam*

The last three years of his Pondicherry stay were a period of unrelieved misery. Acute poverty and unemployment meant a return to the consolations of opium and the attendant miseries of ill health. It was hard to maintain his family. A time came when he did not have enough money to afford a doctor though his child was seriously ill. He would spend whole nights in repeating the word "Shakti." Probably it was this financial worry that ultimately drove Bharati back to India. Far better to suffer in prison alone than witness the daily sufferings of his loved ones. With Bharati, decision meant action. Ten days before the end of the First World War, he left Pondicherry for his wife's place at Kadayam. As soon as he set foot in British India he was arrested, but he was in jail only for three weeks. C.P. Ramaswami Aiyar, Annie Besant, and A. Rangaswamy Iyengar of *Swadesmitran* along with several others exerted their influence and the government released him on the condition that he did not carry on seditious propaganda against the British Indian Government. Iyengar invited him to come back to *Swadesmitran*, but Bharati wished to recuperate in Kadayam for a while.

The village of Kadayam is set in the lovely valley of the River Tamraparni around blue hills crowned with clouds. Bharati was enchanted by the place and started writing again. He was quite 'unorthodox' and mindful of the promise he had given to Sister Nivedita, observed no caste restrictions and ate with people of all castes. He followed no set routine. He shaved when he liked and bathed when he pleased. With just a two-yard loincloth around his waist he would wander about with village urchins, singing and playing games. Although his house was in the Brahmin quarters, there was always a steady stream of visitors with a liberal sprinkling of Muslims and Christians, apart from "untouchables." In his desire to proclaim the equality of the sexes, he would hold the hand of his wife while walking Kadayam's streets. The Brahmins were outraged at such heresy. He flouted tradition in every manner he could. It was considered unclean to touch a donkey. He hugged the animal. With his unkempt hair, long beard, and wild eyes, he did appear mad to Chellamma's friends and relatives.

He paid visits to Madras off and on and also went to quite a few places in Tamil Nadu for delivering lectures. On one of his trips to Madras, he met Mahatma Gandhi for the first and only time in his life. This was how the event came about.

At the end of the First World War, Indians were rewarded not with the bread that they had hoped for, but with the bullets at the notorious Jallianwala Bagh. This provoked a nationwide Civil Disobedience Movement. To feel the pulse of the leaders in different parts of the country, Mahatma Gandhi began to tour India. He came to Madras in March, 1919, and stayed at C. Rajagopalachari's house. One day, Bharati walked in unannounced, startling everyone with his wild appearance. Quickly he walked up to the mattress on the floor where Gandhi was reclining and sat next to him before anybody could stop him. Leaders like C. Rajagopalachari and S. Satyamurti were there along with a few others. The poet did not wait for anybody to introduce him. "Mr. Gandhi! I am going to speak at a meeting in Triplicane beach this evening at 5:30. Could you preside?" Those who were there were so startled by what they considered his rude behavior that they could say nothing. Gandhi was the only calm person in the room. He turned to his secretary, Mahadev Desai, and asked in a gentle voice, "What are my engagements for the day?" Desai replied that Gandhi had a previous commitment and could not go to Bharati's meeting. "Can't you have your meeting tomorrow?" asked Gandhi, turning to Bharati. "No," said the poet shortly, "Good-bye. I bless your efforts. May God help you." So saying he walked out as quickly as he had come. The company that had been stunned by the suddenness of his visit, came to life and there were comments on Bharati's behavior. Those who knew him well nodded sadly.

"Who was that?" inquired Gandhi.

"He is our poet, the poet of our Tamil land who writes beautiful and inspired patriotic songs," said C. Rajagopalachari. Gandhi was silent for a minute. "He should be well looked after. Is there no one in Tamil Nadu to look after him?" These words of Gandhi have been interpreted in a variety of ways. The nearest to the truth seems to be that Gandhi saw at a glance the patriotic fervor and sense of self-confidence in the ragged looking man whose eyes however had an other-worldly gleam. It was in such a spirit that the poet had come to him and Gandhi had realized in a trice the greatness of Bharati. He saw Bharati's anxiousness to have him attend the meeting and the hurt pride his refusal evoked. Bharati would be second to none, not even to Gandhi. In that one gesture the Mahatma had learned his secret.

As regards Bharati's appreciation of Gandhi's greatness, we have proof enough. Apart from showing his admiration in his political articles, Bharati had also hailed the Mahatma in poetic terms. Singing in ecstatic praise of Gandhi:

> You shunned the path of war and murder,
>   Realising the true worth;
> Of the dharmic way to freedom.
>   Shown by great teachers and devotees,
> Realising the fruitfulness of India's
>   New path of satyagraha:
> May the repressions be forgotten
>   And a just life dawn on earth.

Here is proof enough that Bharati the fiery extremist of yesterday was now won over by the new message of Gandhi's nonviolence which the Mahatma had given to his countrymen. This quintessential change in his politics was reflected in his views on other matters also. He had mellowed all round. In his late days he looked like a philosopher, says Rajagopalachari. He did not care when his two requests to the Raja of Ettayapuram for monetary help in publishing all his works in forty volumes, the labors of a life time, were turned down because of the Raja's fear of British anger. Later, he approached a number of people in India to finance the publication of his works, but they, too, failed him.

The negative response from his patrons did seem to affect him. He had spent in all two years at Kadayam planning the publication of his writings. In Pondicherry he had composed poetry at a steady pace, and for one who had come with great hopes from Pondicherry, the apathy of his fellow beings in Tamil Nadu was terribly frustrating. Physically he had become weak and frail, yet his optimism and doggedness were unflinching. With lectures, articles, plans for a new magazine, *Amritam*, Bharati kept himself fully employed. R. A. Padmanabhan has reported that "in his last years Bharati was constantly engaged with the idea of immortality."[10] The name "Amritam" for his projected magazine describes the state of his mind in 1920. In his lectures he introduced his theme and elaborated it. The fearlessness of a yogi is detailed in the poem "To Death" published during the last fortnight of 1919. There he spurns death as a "piece of weed" which he would crush to nothingness itself!

> Death, I look on you as a piece of weed
> Come near — come close,
> So I may crush you
> Beneath my feet.

Although he never doubted that *he* was one of the immortals, his frustration was that this went unacknowledged by his contemporaries. It is a pity that Bharati's conversations never had a Boswell to record them. Like Johnson, Bharati, too, was a scintillating conversationalist, full of wit and humor and satire. An occasional sally remembered by a contemporary shows the treasures we have lost. On the Aryan-Dravidian controversy, for instance, he made the trenchant observation: "My friends! Aryans were preceded by Dravidians, Dravidians by Adi-Dravidians, they by animals and other creatures. We have taken hold of their place and have built houses and farm lands. Suppose these earlier inhabitants turn up demanding their country, all of us will have to go bag and baggage."

The times were not propitious for creative writing. He returned again as an assistant editor, to *Swadesmitran* in Madras in 1920 after having been away for nearly fourteen years — a return to journalism and hackwork. Bharati's genius began to shine anew, and once again he was fully employed. "Once more spirited articles flowed from his pen."[11] Keenly aware of what took place all over the world, he wrote cogently and forcefully on political topics as well as on art and literature. His writings ranged from Greek philosophy and Roman history to Hindu tantric art.

He revived his beach meetings. His patriotic poems were so soul-stirring that he could hold large audiences spellbound for hours — a gift that other public men did not quite relish. He again tried to get his works published and persuaded the *Madras Tamil Sangam* to issue an appeal to the public to help the poet, but there was no response.

Somehow the theme of eternal life haunted him. He began to take an increasing interest in Vedanta and felt he had reached "a complete state of detachment and bliss."[12] But the idyll was too good to last. The clouds had gathered over him unawares and in August, 1921, Bharati went to Karungal Palayam to deliver a lecture entitled "Man has no Death." If one conquered grief, anger, and fear, where then is death, he argued. "It is these that make us die every day, every hour, every minute," he said. One of his last articles to appear in *Swadesmitran*, was an enthusiastic account of Rabindranath Tagore's European travels. Bharati's unfulfilled desire to travel abroad is discernible here.

X   *Death*

One evening, a few days later, Bharati went to the Parthasarthi temple close to his house in Triplicane to feed the temple elephant. It was a daily routine. At that time Bharati was always in the state of seeing the One in all things. To the elephant he proffered the eatables saying, "Brother, I have brought you coconut and fruits." Possibly the elephant was in rut. Whatever the cause, the animal lost his head, picked up the poet with his trunk, and flung him on the ground. There he lay inside the stable almost under the elephant's feet, wounded and unconscious. None dared to approach him for fear of the elephant. But Bharati's friend, Kuvalai Kannan, to whom the news was quickly conveyed, came running. At great personal risk he went into the enclosure and carried the blood-stained Bharati out. He was taken to the Royapettah hospital, and though his general condition was poor, he recovered for a while and even returned to his desk in the newspaper office. However, the toss completely shattered his weak frame, and his attempt to resume his duties cost him dear.

He was presently attacked by dysentery. The frail body that had withstood the accident so recently had already spent all its reserves of strength. Did Bharati realize this? Was that why he refused to take any medicine? Lying in a swoon, he soliloquized in his coma:

> "I am part of Nature, the supreme, the Universal.
> I am one with the cosmos because I am part of Nature. People believe that one goes to heaven after death. But I have been in heaven a long time, for I have seen the truth. Believe me."[13]

It was evening. Through the half closed window the sunlight flecked the floor of his modest Triplicane house. They were alone, Bharati and his wife.

"Chellamma, bring me a mirror."

His wife could not help smiling in spite of her grief. She looked at the graying stubble that hid the deep hollows in his cheeks. The nostrils had already a waxy, deathly pallor. Around the eyes, lines of pain told of the agony of the last few weeks. The skin, outstretched tightly over his hand, looked like a transparent rubber glove. It was obvious to Chellamma that he had taken a dose of his favorite opium, just after recovering from coma.

"Chellamma! Do up my hair and turban and bring me a clean shirt and loincloth."

With tender care his wife lifted him gently out of bed and after a long effort, slow and clumsy, he managed to tidy up himself. He smiled a little weakly. "Chellamma!" He gave her a long pleading look. In it was contained a lifetime of adoration, a world of contrition. He took her hands in his. "I cannot make amends for my faults," he said.

"You have no faults. You are perfect," she flared up.

"My little Chellamma — as sweet as ever. What you needed was care, comfort, and sweet happiness. You are right. You only wanted what every woman craves for. And I — I failed you."

"No, no," said Chellamma between sobs.

"Yes, dear. I am aware how badly I have sinned against you. But I couldn't help it. I could not fight against this that goaded me on to say and do what I did. I know I should have accepted a quiet teacher's job and looked after the family. Instead I was a rolling stone and gave you no peace. I am sorry, Chellamma."

Chellamma could say nothing. She only whispered in a choked voice. "You are tired. Don't talk. Try and sleep." Her cheeks were wet with tears. Gently she raised him a little and tried to settle him more comfortably.

Bharati again fell into a doze, a semiconscious state. His mind seemed quite clear now. He was on his journey and already most of the world ceased to exist. Suddenly he thought of all his unpublished manuscripts. He opened his eyes. "Chellamma!" She bent over him solicitously.

"Chellamma, look after my manuscripts well. They are precious. You may not understand but they are real. Let Nelliyappar and Srinivasachari handle them. One day they'll fetch a lot of money and you'll be comfortable. You shall have your heart's desire."

He could not speak. Again he fell into a coma. It was a dark night. There were no stars. When a few of his close friends came in, Bharati was almost unconscious. At about two in the morning, his friend Parali Nelliyappar had just dozed off when he was startled out of sleep by a loud rattle. The poet's eyes were closed but his lips murmured something. He bent low to catch Bharati's words:

"Mother! Is that you, Mother? Yes, of course. I can see your face." His hands waved in the air. He tried to stretch out his hands to touch her face. "Mother!" he loudly proclaimed. He raised himself for a moment and then fell back dead.

Dawn peeped through the window. It was the September 12, 1921.

For a while his family was in dire straits, but as time passed Bharati's books began to bring in a steady flow of money. In the 1930's *Bharati Prachuralayam*, chiefly managed by Bharati's younger brother Viswanath Iyer, began to publish Bharati's prose and poetry in a number of volumes. At the same time Bharati's patriotic songs rang throughout Tamil Nadu to give a powerful impetus to the freedom movement. In the 1950's the Madras Government obtained the rights to Bharati's works and then made a free gift of them to the people of Tamil Nadu. This in turn encouraged ventures like paperbacks and cheap editions. The passage of time has only emphasized his greatness and the chiseled perfection of his poems. His dreams came true. Today his songs are sung in every private house and are being studied with endless critical attention and appreciation.

The fifty-two years since Bharati's death have shown considerable promise for modern Tamil literature. But a poet greater than he is yet to be born in Tamil Nadu.

CHAPTER 3

Bharati the Poet

SHELLEY has defined poetry as a record of the best and happiest moments of the happiest and best minds; he insists that poetry redeems from decay the visitation of divinity in man. Bharati preeminently satisfies this sublime definition of poetry. His poems are inspired by a divine afflatus with which every line is replete and resonant. To a great extent, Bharati has also proved poetry's incantatory power by using his diction effectively and aphoristically.

Bharati was a poet born to breathe fresh life into the dead bones of a decadent society without losing himself in the childish games of word play and the prejudices of pedantry. With pride in his ancestry and faith in his posterity, he had the poet's perception, the artist's touch, the reformer's zeal, the devotee's faith, the scholar's erudition, the patriot's nationalism, and the cosmopolitan's internationalism. He was a rich blend of the old and the new. He expressed new themes in classic meters, and classic themes in newer modes. Some of his themes are bold and unconventional — so bold that not a few of his contemporaries gasped in wonder, or railed at his temerity.

By every standard Bharati is also the poet of the common man. The language of the common man became in his works the language of poetry. Till then the language of the common man was not the respectable language of high-class literature. One can distinguish throughout the history of the Tamil language two kinds of poetry, one the learned poetry and the other the folk songs. "Bharati was able to blend the two to give it a new form."[1] His poetry broadly falls into three divisions. The first consists of his soul-stirring national songs, which have been sung by millions of Tamilians, who have been roused to patriotic fervor during the past fifty-two years. The second consists of his masterpieces such as *Panchali Sapatham* and *Kuyil Pattu.* In between there is a third division, which comprises religious and philosophic poems and songs. Though these form nearly half his total output, they are not as well known as they should be; for in depth of thought, intensity of emotion, and music of language the poetry found in this division often rises to the level of his masterpieces. It is "infinitely superior to that of his national songs, but did not attain so much popularity because of its limited appeal."[2]

I   *National Songs*

The poet who exercised the greatest influence on him during his early period was Shelley, since it was he who dared declare that "poets are the unacknowledged legislators of mankind." Bharati loved Shelley's tireless search for individual liberty. Returning to Ettayapuram from Benares, Bharati slowly got saturated with, and steeped in, Shelley. For he found in him a much needed intellectual stimulus.

Coming to Madras, Bharati saw that there was a far-flung public of intellectuals whom he could address in a serious, responsible, and truly committed manner. The fit audience was ready. Like other parts of the country, Tamil Nadu too had begun having newspapers and periodicals to disseminate new political and social thought. But prose could not appeal to the rational element in the people, while poetry could electrify them and make heroes out of common clay. He began by turning the minds of his countrymen to the ideal of freedom and employed all the capacity of a poet for mood and expression. He could be sad and moving like Conte Giacomo Leopardi, intoning a dirge over the glory of the past, or he could speak of it in such rousing accents that the accumulated wisdom and strength of the ages came to life in the passing moment, giving it the irresistible validity of the eternal. He could lash out furiously at the indifference, self-seeking, meanness of his countrymen with a biting irony like Heinrich Heine's. He could be assured and serene like Swami Vivekananda, affirming with boundless faith his country's great destiny. "In the national struggle for freedom, while politicians were fighting against British law and statute and armed might, Bharati fought the harder fight against the langor of the spirit."[3] He gave the Tamilians the vision without which a people perish and the will without which a vision is but an idle dream. No wonder to this day he is still, to the Tamilians, primarily the *Desiya Kavi*, the Nationalist Poet.

In 1907 V. Krishnaswami Iyer printed and distributed fifteen thousand copies of three patriotic songs by Bharati. There was an unprecedented demand for more such poems. Two volumes of poetry followed and were instantaneous successes. *Swadesa Gitangal* (1908) contained fourteen songs. Introducing them, the poet wrote, "I offer these flowers at the feet of Mother Bharat who is a symbol of unity and youthfulness. I well know that my flowers have no scent. Did not Lord Siva accept the stones thrown by a low born person? Even so, may Mother Bharat accept my flowers with kindness!"

There was no need for such an apology. Tamilians at once recognized the genius revealed in the songs, and they asked only for more of them, Bharati released *Janma Bhoomi* in 1909. He said in the foreword that "Because of my love for the light of freedom I placed some poetic flowers at Mother's feet. To my pleasant surprise, devotees found them to be good. Mother accept my offerings. By the confidence born of it, I have brought some more flowers for Mother's feet."

Bharati continued to write poems on patriotism to the end of his life. It is a fairly large collection. Some are descriptive, some satirical, others idealistic, and some even nostalgic. There is thus tremendous variety, but the Bharati touch is everywhere, the touch that transformed the mundane market quality of politics into the glowing gold of immortal poetry.

He abjured mere politics and propaganda. The political freedom that Bharati sings of is not simply the driving out of the British; it is synonymous with social equality and economic justice. To him freedom was an elemental thirst, a basic aspiration and need of the human soul. Bharati's was the religion of patriotism advocated by prophets like Tilak and Sri Aurobindo, not etherealized into a vague notion of world brotherhood, but a condition of commitment that gives vital nurture to man, a sense of "belonging" and self-respect. He was full of admiration for Tilak, who said "Swaraj [Independence] is my birth right." With such commitment, Bharati could aspire, suffer, demand, and exult as a citizen of a particular country conscious of his civil and human rights. His ebullition of anger, like the hiss of a snake, is proverbially recited with the taut energy of a shackled giant in "Vande Mataram" and "Jaya Bharata." Here is an example of his concentrated passion and crystalline verse, to which no English rendering can do justice:

> Mother, we bow to thee,
> Victorious Mother,
> We bow to thee!

Jai Hind! Jai Bharat!
Victory to Bharat!
Victory! Victory!   Mother, we bow.

Men, women, gods
Of Aryavarta
Sing in chorus
The exultant chant   Mother, we bow.

Anguished in mind,
Shrivelled in body,
The patriots still
Cry from the depths   Mother, we bow.

Be victory ours
Or defeat and death,
We stand united
And raise the chant   Mother, we bow.

The concept of a united India as the Mother who sustains her children is nothing new for India. Although divided into the North and South by the Vindhya mountains, there is no doubt that the culture of the country has been essentially one. This concept was prevalent even in the Vedic age. In Radha Kumad Mookerji's words, the fundamental unity of India "was not a mere intellectual conception or an abstract idea but a vivid realization through the heart: not the happy hit of a momentary inspiration but the settled habit of national thought induced by religious texts and daily prayers."[4] Towards the close of the last century, Bankim Chandra Chatterji wrote a novel called *Ananda Math*. In the course of the text he inserted a hymn to Mother India. The opening line was "Vande Mataram." This hymn became famous during the agitation against the Partition of Bengal. In Sri Aurobindo's words:

The mantra [incantation] had been given and in a single day a whole people had been converted to the religion of patriotism. The Mother had revealed Herself. Once that vision had come to a people, there can be no rest, no peace, no further slumber till the temple has been made ready, the image installed and the sacrifice offered.

Subramanya Bharati took up the task of raising this temple in the hearts of the Tamils. He approached the work from three directions: an incantatory review of India, detailing its physical and spiritual greatness; an injection of the ideal of "freedom" into every person so as to banish fear; and an evocation of the lives of the great men of India as living examples for emulation. Bharati thus wrote poems of description, of exhortation, and of heroic portraiture.

One of Bharati's early poems, "Salutation to India," states with winning homeliness the reasons for his love of the Motherland:

> This, this is the land that saw
>   Father and mother live and thrive in joy;
> This the land where numberless ancestors
>   Lived their hoary lives and died.
> Thoughts a thousand grew
>   And flourished in this land.
> In remembrance of it all
>   May I not praise my land,
> And singing time and again:
>   Mother, I bow to thee!
>   Mother, I bow to thee!

Subramanya Bharati shares with his fellow nationals his "sense of exultation at the greatness of India and his feeling of love and reverence to the Mother."[5] India is truly the best country in all this wide world:

> In knowledge and yogic trance,
>   Self respect and charity,
> In music and honeyed poesy —
>   India is the best among nations,
> In heroism and warrior strength,
>   In pity and helpfulness,
> In doubling experience with thought —
>   India shines resplendent.

The poem is a prolonged paean to India's greatness. When Bharati was composing his songs, Indians were forgetting their noble heritage and adapting themselves to English civilization, English education, and English customs. Indians increasingly felt that it was degrading to speak in their own mother tongue. The land was at its lowest ebb and in an appalling condition. But Bharati made this bold affirmation:

> Fearless warriors have lived here,
> Many a sage has sanctified this land;

> The divinest music has been heard here,
> And all auspicious things here are found.
> Here Brahma knowledge has taken root,
> And the Buddha preached his dharma here;
> Of hoary antiquity is India,
> She is peerless, let us praise her!

Whatever the half-educated and ill-educated might say would not affect *Her* glory or greatness. India is eternal. In "Jaya Bharata" he sings:

> She won a hundred lands
>   By thought's creative power.
> Let even the ungodly come
>   To enrich her now,
> Let searing poverty
>   Reduce her to defeat;
> Dharma she'll not abjure.
>   Hail Mother!

Mother India, eternally fresh and rich in knowledge, a power and personality supreme, undaunted by defeat, sustains dharma. She holds on to truth in spite of foreign exploitation. She enriches our culture, even if we should be apathetic; she keeps her bowls filled, even when we denude her of her riches; she teaches us the love of freedom, even though we may indulge in slavish orgies. All history and legend and myth, all hope and striving and achievement, all the dreams and poets and all the visions of seers — all are comprehended in the Mother. It was her hands that fashioned the *Vedas* and she who taught the *Gita.* It was she who spoke the words of the Buddha. All qualities are found in Her yet She stands as the only Truth. She unifies all contradictions; She integrates all differences.

> She has three hundred million faces,
>   But her heart is one;
> She speaks eighteen languages,
>   Yet her mind is one.

Bharati was sure that, when the call came, India's millions would answer with one voice. Freedom for this variegated yet unified India was the golden bough. Whatever the impediment, this unity should be preserved. An extremist in politics though he was, Bharati never surrendered to the all too common revolutionary propensity to destroy. He did not like the bitter destructive way to freedom. He did his best to awaken the passion for freedom and the consciousness of equality and unity in a land torn for centuries by foreign rule and sharp caste divisions. A famous song of his sung all over the Tamil land in the days of the nationalist struggle runs:

> Freedom, freedom, freedom!
> To the Pariahs, to the Tiyas, to the Pulayas,
> freedom!
> To the Paravas, to the Kuravas, to the Maravas,
> freedom!
> Come, let us labor all,
> Sparing naught and hurting none,
> Walking in the way of Truth and Light,
> There shall be none of low degree,
> And none shall be oppressed.
> Born in India, all are of noble birth
> Wealth and learning — may they flourish,
> With joy of mind, let us live
> Like brothers all alike
> Perish ignorance!
> In man and woman, alike,
> No more of subordination.
> In every walk of life equality.
> Man and woman shall equal be
> In this land of ours.
> Freedom, freedom, freedom!
> To the Pariahs, to the Tiyas, to the Pulayas,
> freedom.
> To the Paravas, the Kuravas, the Maravas,
> freedom![6]

Bharati could love even an enemy: "hatred" is a word he did not understand. He would pray to God to effect a change of heart in his enemies, but he could not hate them. In this he was a true forerunner of Gandhi. It was Bharati's absolute faith in God that freed him from the sin and sickness of hate. He cajoles the Lord in many ways to free his country, and the Lord he invokes in his patriotic poems is always Krishna. That divine-human figure poised between the Pandava and Kaurava armies on the field of Kurukshetra: who but He can help India in bondage?

Love thine enemy, heart of mine, Oh!
Love thine enemy.
Hast thou not seen the shining flame
Amidst the darkening smoke?
In foeman's soul lives Krishna, whom
As Love the wise invoke.

But Bharati's free India was to be wrought, not through bloodshed, but through peaceful means, the democratic means of conscious will and determined action, through force of persuasion and disciplined organization. Bharati loved the country too much to allow it to be ruined by pointless bloodshed. His *Bharat Mata Navaratna Malai* is a sequence of nine lyrics, anticipating the peaceful revolution that was to be launched by Gandhi.

Till now the unrighteous war mongers
Wore sin as a burnished crown
And shamelessly affirmed
That Might is Right.
War lords had their murderous armies
To sustain their law of Might.
To-day
India shows the other countries
A new way.
The world famous Tagore.
King of poets,
Says ringingly:
"In this wide world
The leader of all men
Is Mohandas Gandhi
The image of dharma."
With Gandhi as our leader
We to prove are prepared
That dharma alone succeeds
In politics, as in all things. . . .
Chant victory! Blow the white conch!

It was fortunate that Bharati's sane voice was raised against violence in politics. The cult of violence in any case made little appeal to people in Madras. Tamilnadu never had, like Bengal or Maharashtra, to contend with organized or large-scale terrorism. Bharati, although an avowed extremist, never encouraged terrorist activities. "He preferred to convince his people of the greatness of India's past and to exhort them to recreate that golden age in the present. He found the current situation depressing, the mass of people apathetic."[8]

In Bharati's own words:

> The heart can stand this no more —
>   Look at these will-less folk,
> Frightened, ah! there's nothing
>   They do not fear.
>
> Imagining ghosts, they cry —
>   On this tree, in that tank!
> It's lurking here, they shout.
>   Of their own thoughts they die of fear.

The poet's anger comes out in measured gasps to exorcise the ghosts that have all but emasculated India into a spiritless and slavish nation. The total effect is overwhelming, and the listener is forced into a mood of self-laceration. However, Bharati also sees prophetically a resurgent India and thus welcomes the "India to Be":

> Come, come thou with victory in your grasp
> Come, come thou modest in speech;
> Come, thou full grown to manhood, come,
> Come, thou of face immaculate, come.
> Come, come thou and turn thought into deed,
> Come, come thou whose will is equal to desire;
> Come, come take up the mighty task
> Of forging the unity of our land.

In the mind's eye Bharati sees this shining new race of Indians, comprising the freedom loving Rajasthanis, Maharashtrians, Bengalis, Andhras, Tamils, Mysorians and the rest, gathering together below the flag of India fluttering in the breeze.

But this visionary was also a stern realist. Bharati saw clearly the conditions that had to be established if freedom was to come and remain. Condemning the caste system he writes: "We are of the same caste and race, / We are children of India all; / We are equal in law and stature, / And everyone is India's king." "He envisioned his free India as a social democracy consisting of responsible, self-poised and self-perfecting individuals."[9] His best poem on the theme is "India a vision of the future." He would have us defeat hatred, kill fear, and build the new India. "We'll stroll upon silvery Himalayas, / Our ships will sail upon all the seas . . . / We'll bring the water from Bengal's rivers / And irrigate the lands of the South." Bharati was thus a constructive patriot, and no mere weaver of wayward fancies.

Apart from whispering (and sometimes dinning) into his listeners' ears the grandeur and the good that was India and presenting the Indian subcontinent as a totality of experience and as a human-divine personality, Bharati also tried to teach his countrymen the nature and implications of freedom. "Freedom" is an incandescent and holy word for Bharati. His freedom is an absolute thing, not to be modified by adjectives like "political" or "social" or "economic." It is real freedom from all shackles — birdlike, wavelike, ethereal freedom. There is nothing higher, and hence this "freedom" is worth all one's sacrifices. "Political independence was an immediate first step, but a 'free' person was the ultimate ideal."[10] Patriotism when crudely applied to a local situation might take the form of mere suicidal defiance. The same emotion, however, when consistently applied in all developing situations lead to the real state of liberty. From local patriotism grows the ideal of universal freedom — hence the prayer to liberty:

> Though torn away from the warmth of home,
> In prison cell I pine,
> Though rank and wealth do fade and leave
> Reproaches only mine,
> Though griefs on griefs crowd without end
> And shake and shatter me,
> Oh! Liberty, never would I
> Forget to bow to thee.

What if the whole world were yours, but you were denied liberty of the soul? Rich persons living in wealthy countries are often no better than corpses. Only by seraphically "living" persons can the nation be truly enriched:

> Could it be called a land
> The land bereft of liberty's light?
> What strength is there, what knowledge, zeal,
> What spirit, wisdom bright?
> What poetry, scriptures, or what arts,
> Cherished and divine?
> Liberty, they, have sinned who have lost

> The good that's only thine
> Their sickness grows on them, they lose
> The fire that is life's zest.

The song is set to a lilting tune and these verses have played a notable and decisive role in diffusing the ideal of an egalitarian society among the masses. He repeatedly invokes the Goddess of Liberty to bless his land and people with the gift of true freedom, which should embrace *all* living things. Bharati's ideal, then, is an ultimate democracy which he tried all his life to teach his fellow countrymen. It is easy to fashion a democratic constitution; but to make democracy work, to retain the reality of freedom for all, is an arduous but necessary task. For this reason Bharati urged fearlessness, for only the fearless can be truly free. Many of his songs dwell on this theme:

> Chant India's name,
> Defeating hatred,
> Killing fear!
> Beat! Beat the drum!
> Beat the drum of victory!
> Having vanquished the demon fear.
> And killed the reptile Lie.
> We have embraced the Veda's path
> That leads to Brahma-knowledge.

His most famous poem on fearlessness ends "Should the very Heavens fall on my head, / Flinch not! There is no fear."

Bharati proceeded to give examples of such fearlessness. "Chatrapati Shivaji," an unfinished poem of 187 lines, is a long oration by Shivaji, the Maratha warrior, in the tone of a ringing war cry. Bharati summarizes the whole of the *Gita* in a few lines of great power. There is another long poem on the Sikh Guru Gobind Singh that describes the birth of the Khalsa (Sikh Order) at the convention at Anandpur, Punjab.

> Mere knowledge makes no men,
> The true living person is he who
> Shows his mettle for dharma's sake.
> To spot out such heroes
> In that assembled millions
> He committed this dire experiment.

Five such self-less warriors are enough
To give hope for the future day.
He returned with the five "victims"
Alive and well to the assembled ones.
Shouts of wonder rose to the sky.

Bharati wished to have such a race of people all over India. He saw
the beginnings of such a new race in the country's leaders led by
Gandhi. With a poet's intuition, Bharati foresaw the force of Gandhi.
His five-stanza poem on Gandhi sums up Gandhi's later career, with
remarkable percipience and is a gem among Bharati's patriotic
poems: "How shall we praise thee? / As one whose choicest
herbs / Healed the cobra's bite? / As one who held the hill as
cover?"

In his faith in a unified India, in his passion for freedom and liberty and admiration for national leaders, Bharati did not neglect his
region either. While condemning linguistic chauvinism, he loved his
mother tongue with a total love. He knew several languages, but
Tamil held the first place in his heart. He demonstrated how the
language could be made to express the subtlest nuances of modern
knowledge: "Of the many languages we know / None is as sweet as
Tamil! / Let us make honey-sweet Tamil / Ring through the
world!" Bharati exhorts his people to "develop Tamil according to a
planned schedule."[11] This would include translations of foreign
classics into Tamil, encouraging creative writing in Tamil, and
translating Tamil classics into foreign languages so that they would
reach a worldwide audience. His greatest contribution to Tamil was
not praising it in beautiful lyrics but *writing* it and giving it a new life.
He was a forceful writer in English and had good command of
Sanskrit, but his first love and living breath was Tamil.

II   *Major Works*

"If poetry comes not as naturally as leaves of a tree, it had better
not come at all," said Keats. To Bharati poetry came as "naturally
as leaves of a tree," a fact which does not make his poetry staccato or
appear "anaemic and constipated," to use Aldous Huxley's
diagnostic words from a different context. He is a poet with a
genuine passion for poetry. More than a poet Bharati was a singer.
In his three major works — *Kannan Pattu* (Song of Krishna), *Kuyil
Pattu* (Song of the Cuckoo), and *Panchali Sapatham* (Panchali's
Vow), his poetry has not merely the tidal movement of rhythm that

all poetry should have, but the wave beats of a song that are direct and simple creating a shining interspace between word and word. "I sing," he says simply, "because I have drunk deep of the ambrosial wine blended of the moonlight, stars and the wind." But he brews the wine himself in the vats of his intuition which make his masterpieces "passing sweet to the eye." These three masterpieces of Bharati are rich with the sights and sounds of the earth — the red laugh of the wild flower on the ash heap, the swinging dart of the sparrow, morning light filling the grassland, "a flood of molten gold, sweet as honey," the palm branch swaying and waking silver ripples in the moonlight, the long, long snake basking in the sun, rivers swinging down to the sounds of their own music, the tiger testing its voice in the gamut of terror, the friendly roundelays of birds, the fiercely glad tumult of the monsoon. Writing with his eye on the object and with an unerring sense of the emotive or picturesque detail, Bharati revived the poet's fidelity to nature and yet in his descriptions, there is a fairy light, indefinable and elusive, a Merlin's gleam flashing behind the veil. It is not the beauty of leaf or flower, of the world of eye and ear that is of primary moment to Bharati. It is the spirit of infinite loveliness running like fire beneath the coloured ash of appearance that he touches; and in one ecstatic moment, Beauty and Truth become one and we are made aware of "the loveliness of pure nature / Scooping deep into the billowy ocean / True nectar, healer of wounds and maker of delights / Source of light and force like soma wine."

Surely Bharati has profited a great deal by the accumulated wisdom of India's poets and prophets of old. "He is much impressed with the negative capability and the fine artistic temper of Thiruvalluvar, the majestic march of Kamban's immortal verse, the serene lofty sweep of his range of ideas in the realm of thought. He is saturated with (and steeped in) Kalidas who cast a profound spell on him. It is no exaggeration to say that the streams of culture of these three poets flow harmoniously in Bharati."[12]

Blending the old and new he pours the rich wine of his experiences into the old bottles of India's poetic traditions. Like many a modern author he has pressed into his services old situations for creating new patterns of thought and experience. None may deny the supreme fact that poets flourish only in the rich soil of tradition; and the individual talent is like a mounting wave against the vast background of an inexhaustible sea of traditions. Tagore in his essay *What is Art* has brought home to us this aspect so admirably reflected in Bharati.

III   *Kannan Pattu*

Bharati's best dramatic improvizations on a lyrical base are elaborately worked out in his *magnum opus* known as the Kannan songs. They are twenty-three in number and they play delectable variations on a single theme. The collection was first published in 1917, with a preface by Parali Nellaiyappa Pillai. The style of the lyrics is simple and summons the sensuous, and the meaning steals into us as naturally as the notes of a nightingale in spring. Of all the incarnations of Vishnu, that of Krishna as God is considered to be the most complete. It has appealed most powerfully to popular imagination and called forth not only several Puranas, including the famous *Bhagavatha,* but also the most moving songs of earlier Tamil poets like Perialwar and Kulasekhara Alwar. In other Indian languages also, Lord Krishna has been the darling of several poets and composers. Jayadeva's *Gita Govindam* and Lila Sukhar's *Krishnakarnamritham* in Sanskrit and Mirabai's songs in Hindi are supreme instances of lyrical poems and perhaps unrivaled as musical classics. Lord Krishna is thus the beau ideal of Indian erotic art no less than of its mystic poetry; and Bharati paints him as "lover, friend, disciple, teacher, father, mother and mistress and in many other human relationships."[13]

> The lass pines for her Krishna
> His lovely face slips from memory
> To whom shall I wail my friend
> My heart feels his love, yet,
> How could I forget his face.

How could she, for "Bees forgetting honey, / Flower forgetting light / Plants forgetting rain, / Happen not on earth my friend."

Here Tagore's summation is relevant. "Lord Krishna is the eternal bridegroom and we are his bride. In India the greatest part of her Literature is religious because God with the Indians is not a distant God. He belongs to their homes as well as to their temple. His nearness is felt in all the human relationship of love and affection and in all festivities. He is the chief guest who is honored. In seasons of flowers and fruits, in the coming of the rain, in fullness of the autumn, the hem of His mantle is seen and His footsteps heard. He is worshipped in all the true objects of worship and is loved wherever Love is true. He is known in the man and woman who is true. In children, He is born again and again, the Eternal Child. Therefore

India's religious songs are her love songs."[14] Bharati shows the inseparable union of the lovers in a string of wonderful similies which have a magical effect:

> Rain that singeth, thou to me,
> Peacock dancing, I to thee;
> Thou to me the juice of grape,
> And I to thee the cup agape
> O spotless beauty, Krishna bright,
> Perennial fount of deep delight,
> O Love, thy face hath grown divine,
> For there the deathless truth doth shine.

This poem "Kannan En Kulandai," the most famous of his Kannan songs and the summit of Tamil poetry, has several stanzas which conclude with the following:

> As life to pulse and gold to rings,
> As star to planet, soul to things,
> So Krishna, Love, art thou to me,
> Thou the Force, I the Victory:
>   and all the joys of Heaven and Earth.
> In thee, O Krishna, have their birth,
> Eternal glory, endless might,
> O heart of mine, O divine light.

This is a novel approach to God and shows that love dares anything and God is everywhere and in everything. Bharati's faith was of such intensity that he lived in Krishna constantly, and hence his lyrics on Krishna move us to our depths. Bharati flaunts no scholarship here; nor are these lyrics molded of cloying praise. Carping critics may demur that it is all a little stale, but such criticism is hardly fair. "Bharati has proved what every reader of poetry always knew, that if a poet is equal to his task, he can invest an old theme with a new significance and beauty by his poetic emotion and artistic skill."[15] Bharati's musical liveliness and uninhibited imagery are essentially his own and give his superb collection an ineffable charm. In revealing the celestial glory of childhood in human precincts the paternal and maternal affection finds a most enjoyable expression indeed. The divine innocence of children, who are not yet affected by the poisonous shadows of the human world, is painted in an exalted manner.

My little, flitting bird;
My soul's dear treasury;
Thou dost uplift my life
To pride from misery.

Sweet infant dew of love!
Image of living gold!
Honey, that tripping comes
That I may thee enfold!

My soul leaps in delight
To see thee steeped in me;
And flies out to embrace
Thee frisking merrily.

A kiss upon thy brow
With pride doth make me swell;
With thrills I listen, when
Of thee my neighbors tell.

Thy cheek against my lips,
Is to my heart like wine.
Sweet frenzy 'tis to hold
Thee close, O darling mine.

His poetic medium is so natural, thrilling and transparent indeed. In love or war Krishna is indispensable and ever helpful to his friend. At the same time he is no friend to the false hearted, or the proud, or those who do not hold fast to truth.

"*Krishna My Mother*" has a poignancy about it; Bharati's mother had died when he was very young. The poet asks, "Do tomes tell tales as sweet as yours? / In giving love which god can equal you?" The poet enables us to realize the many splendored glory of the one God, his divinity as well as humanity and his true nature that transcends divisions of sex and age. Sex in *Kannan Pattu* has nothing physical about it in Bharati's mystic language. "The Absolute is all sorts of relationship and there need arise no shock at this poetic characterization as the lady love, once the physical and sexual ideas are divorced from our mind."[16] Bharati dramatizes the longing, the quest and the ultimate realization for the benefit of the reader. The search, the "dark night of the soul," and the vision are all masterfully mirrored in "*Krishna My Beloved.*"

Like the worm in the angler's line,
Like a flame in the wind,
My heart did throb in anguish
A long, long while.
Like a caged parrot
I sorrowed alone.
Even the sweetest things
Turned bitter on my tongue
Once as I dreamt
In my sleep
An utter stranger
Touched my heart;
As I woke with a start,
He disappeared:
Only then did my heart
Tingle with joy.
I thrilled to my roots,
Dear Friend;
Health came back; and home,
Once more a place of comfort,
Wore a fresh happy look,
And I loved one and all;
Fear fled from me,
And Beauty came.
As I sensed again in thought
The cool, soft touch,
The body thrilled anew
And a strange peace was mine,
I wondered in my mind
Who he might have been!
Lo! there the form of Krishna
Stood before my eyes.

The devotee's search for the Deity is given the immediacy of drama in another poem titled "Beloved." She searches for Krishna in a dense forest and is accosted by a lustful hunter. The finale leaves us wondering. Was the hunter an illusion destroyed by the appearance of Krishna? Or was he Krishna Himself come to tease her and test her faith?

In this poem we have a minuteness of detail, a richness of color, and quivering lyrical movement which recall to us the pre-Raphaelite school of a William Morris or Dante Gabriel Rossetti. Bharati goes on piling image upon image in such a manner that the "Beloved"

series ends with "an anticlimax,"[17] with the divine pathos of forgetting *what*, while remembering *how*, one had felt:

> Forgotten is the face beloved —
> Ah! my friend! Dare I say this?
> The heart has not forgot the love —
> Yet how could mind forget the face?

Love in its purest form needs no image to keep it alive.

Again, Krishna becomes the quintessence of womanhood —
woman in her glamor, goodness, and glory. She is the shy maid over-
taken by the stormy impetuosity of the lover. Or she merges into
Nature and is found everywhere:

> In the heaving sea I saw your face,
> And in the azure sky;
> In that thick foam I saw your face,
> And in these tiny bubbles;
> Searching every inch of cloud,
> I found your face and nothing else.
> Hearing running laughter at my back,
> I pushed aside your hands
> And turned behind to find only your face.

This series on Krishna as the lady love culminates in the poem where
the "I-You" contradiction is resolved in the kinship that restores
wholeness to the parts. The One alone remains in the apparent many.
It is indeed a daring innovation in the treatment of love. "The
realization of God in all things by the vision of Divine Love is
characteristically Indian."[18] In "Love Mad," the mother of a love-
stricken girl (symbolizing the human soul yearning to merge into the
Godhead) is complaining to her friend of the sad plight of the child,
whom love for Krishna has rendered "mad"; the effect of the
"madness" is that in all things she is able to see nothing but forms of
Krishna, the ultimate spirit of the Universe.

> Where tumblers dance with their pots,
> She runs and cries 'Krishna.'
> At the charming notes of a flute she faints,
> For "Krishna, He playeth."
> When cowherd dames bring butter,
> She is sure it was tasted by Him.

All helpless am I, my friends
My child has He rendered mad.

Kannan Pattu is thus a harmony of various notes. It is as though
God Himself has descended into clay to transform this earth-life into
the life divine. Krishna is the Vedic Seer, the one true friend, who
removes all the corrosive cares of life. When he falls on the thorns of
life and bleeds, Krishna pours into his heart healing balm of His wise
and wholesome counsel. God as a Mother envelops the infinite book
of nature. God as his Father is a poet from whose mighty lyre has
flowed the epic song of creation. He is old, yet ever new; and time
writes no wrinkles on the eternal brow of the Lord. Lord as He is, He
walks amongst the lowliest and the lost, Krishna plays the part of an
ideal servant. Unlike the ordinary servant of the earth who indulges
in a tissue of lies, he is the very pink and pattern of truth and service.
He is a great King who waits patiently and watches the sinful deeds
of men on earth. His mills grind slowly but surely. In Him the terrible and the beautiful meet and mingle. The song which flows from
Krishna's divine flute suddenly turns into the blare of a trumpet, calling men to fierce battle. God as an ideal student is delighted in seeing
Himself in diverse relationships to the objects of his study and
worship. Krishna alone is a teacher who can lift the heavy burden of
our lives. In Him is our peace. As a child, Krishna is indeed a unique
conception. Only as a child one can enter the Kingdom of God. The
divine Krishna comes to the poet like the dancing wave of honey. It
suggests to him a breathing image of gold. But ever Krishna remains
the elusive reality. After having exhausted all these human ap-
proaches, Bharati has a vision of Krishna as the Supreme Creatrix.
All doubts, ecstasies, anger, fears, and cares are resolved in the peace
of absolute surrender: "I take refuge in Thee! Krishna my Mother, /
In Thee I take refuge."

IV *Panchali Sapatham*

Bharati described his verse drama as but a translation of some
episodes in Vyasa's *Mahabharata*. This is true enough. All the
episodes — the dice game, the righteous stand of Vikarna, the insult
to Panchali (Draupadi), Bhima's explosive anger, and Arjuna's
mollifying reply — are in the original. But Bharati gives to these
events and characters a modern touch and a topical slant. His aim is
to create a poem of epic magnitude in modern Tamil, avoiding the
punditry and obscurantism of the middle ages and using instead

"simple phrases, simple style, easily understood prosody, rhythm liked by the common man."

Panchali Sapatham (Panchali's vow) consists of 2548 lines of which about 1950 lines are in the nature of a monologue or dialogue. Of the rest, nearly 200 lines treat the description of the land and people of Hastinapur, the stage on which the action takes place. The remaining 400 lines are in the form of comments by the poet himself lamenting and using scathing irony about the actions of the characters. In all, the work is of twenty-four verses in the form of a verse drama. The 600 lines, apart from the monologue or dialogue, seem not to fit this verse form but out of these about 400 lines are of the ideal form to be recited by a chorus as in the world masterpieces, especially the Greek tragedies. This chorus will be more Euripidean in nature than Aeschylean. And as in ancient Greek literature some of these passages suited for a chorus are excellent. The 200 lines dealing with the land and people of Hastinapur along with the invocation to gods are but a prologue as is common in a great many verse dramas and are recitable from behind the curtain before it rises.

The first part of *Panchali Sapatham* appeared in 1912, the second part twelve years later. Although Bharati's drama concentrates on a single crisis in the *Mahabharata,* yet this is the pivot of Vyasa's epic, and the most dramatic moment in *Mahabharata.* This crisis was the seed of the great war that destroyed many of the royal princes in India. In this thrilling drama, written in his inimitable modern style and with limpid words, we see the clash of personalities — the greedy Duryodhana, the wily Sakuni, the dotard Dhritharashtra, the noble Vidura, the ineffective Bhishma, the brutish Duschasana, the sedate Yudhistira, the fiery Bhima, and a succession of other poignant personalities. All the earlier events lead the reader to the terrible moment when Duschasana rises to disrobe Panchali. The reader holds his breath for an instant, then the miracle occurs, and life resumes its routine rhythms. But for the contending parties themselves this crisis is the point of no return. The events that follow, including the great Kurukshetra war, inevitably and remorselessly flow out of that moment. By pouncing on this moment and linking it to the earlier motivations of Duryodhana and the later series of "vows" that seal his fate, Bharati created an architecturally perfect poem that has both epic sweep and the intensity of tragic drama.

The drama consists of five cantos. The first, "Duryodhana's Plot," begins with a prayer. We see the city of Hastinapur in all its prosperity. Soon we reach Duryodhana's court and catch a glimpse of evil thoughts seething in his heart. The cancer is the sin of envy: "In the gaze of manly Arjuna / Who wields the Gandiva bow: / And on giant Bhima's shoulders, too, / My shame is seen: O woe is me!" From childhood Duryodhana had been envious of the Pandava brothers, especially Bhima. The *Rajasuva* sacrifice had been a tremendous success. Duryodhana's heart refused to forget its glory.

> As when the fire from earth's deep center
> Boils and makes way to the crust
> And its great heat melts the rock
> And the lava flows and spreads;
> The volcano envy in his heart
> Erupted in his mind and soul.
> All strength and manliness melted,
> Valor and honor were lost.

He goes whispering to his uncle Sakuni and pleads for revenge by hook or crook. Above all the slights real or imaginary, Duryodhana's greatest humiliation had come from the innocent laughter of Panchali when she had seen him topple down and swoon on the marble floor. She and the Pandava brothers must be reduced to beggary and cast on the streets! Sakuni suggests a game of dice. Dhritarashtra tries to stop this obviously immoral thing, but Duryodhana, like a feverish person venting his spleen upon the doctor, raises his voice against his aged father. The old king bemoans the developing tragedy but allows things to take their own course. Despite Vidura's appeal not to fall into the trap Yudhisthira accepts the challenge in a philosophical mood. In the name of "duty" he leads his brothers to the dice game at Hastinapur.

The second canto, "The Game of Dice," shows the Pandava Prince systematically denuded of all his possessions. Vidura's wise words go unheeded. The Pandavas attribute their failings to the power of fate and, though forewarned, move towards the tragic climax. This brings out the wrath of the poet in great speech: "Were there no fools on this earth / Before you were born? Were all the men seers who lived / Before you?"

In the third canto, we find the Pandavas losing their personal liberty as a result of the game, and reaching the nadir of their fortunes. At last Panchali, their wife, is herself made a pawn. The fourth canto, "The insult to Panchali," opens with a poignant note: "Would one kill a dear child / For leather to make sandals? / For the dicing between angered Princes / Should Panchali be the pawn?" It is a terrible heart rending scene — the Pandavas, horrified and helpless; Duryodhana and his group exulting in their "victory"; Vidura arguing and cursing in vain; and the evil Kaurava Princes, yelling for the "slave" Panchali. And so we come to the final canto, "The Vow." Panchali is dragged by her tresses to the Kuru Court by Duschasana. A question is posed by Panchali to Duschasana whether she was lost by her husband after he lost himself, in which event, he himself being a slave, had no possessions and therefore, had no right to dispose of her. Duschasana was, of course, in no mood to answer questions and Panchali is dragged through the streets. Not a single Kshatriya hand is raised in her defense. The populace that thronged the thoroughfares did not raise a finger on the side of righteousness. The poet calls them "Curs, without a semblance of manliness, / The beastly prince should have been destroyed / and the lady restored to her dignity. / They stood, instead like tall trees / and lamented." Such was the popular degradation, but what about the leaders? The joy of Duryodhana and his brood knows no bounds. At the court, the Pandava Princes, too, sat like dummies with bowed heads.

Panchali addressing everybody at the court, cries

> You, who before the sacred fire,
> Vowed to honor me.
> You, who have performed many a penance
> and Yagnas,
> You, who have duty to stand up against
> Injustice.
> All of you are dumb and do not stop
> this wretch.

The Pandavas, the other princes and sages are indeed dumb. Bhishma, alone, tries to answer, but what an apology to one who was righteousness itself. He says:

> In days of yore
> The sexes were equal.
> But times have changed;
> Woman is inferior.
> A wife can be sold,
> Or gifted like cattle.
> Dharma sanctions
> Your sale as a slave.
> I know what they do here

Is repugnant beyond measure.
But Sastras and customs
Are alike against you.
Impotent am I to halt this evil.

Panchali answers:

Finely, bravely spoken, Sir!
When treacherous Ravana, having carried away
And lodged Sita in his garden,
Called his ministers and law givers
And told them the deed he had done,
These same wise advisers declared:
"Thou hast done the proper thing:
"Twill square with dharma's claims!"
When a demon king rules the land,
Needs must the Shastras feed on filth! . . .
O ye that have sisters and wives,
Isn't this a crime on Woman?
Would you all be damned for ever?
Pity my plight!

Bhima alone raises his voice against this outrage. Legally a slave, he has no right to turn his wrath on the Kaurava hordes. Besides, according to him, the Dharma-loving Yudhishthira with his passion for "gambling," is the cause of Panchali's woe. So he tells his younger brother; "We shall bear it no longer: / Bring a torch, Sahadev! / Yudhishthira's hand played the losing stakes / We'll burn his hand away!" But cool-headed Partha replies:

Bhima, the fire of your anger has
Covered with its smoke your Intelligence.
You abuse our Lord.
But an example are we at this moment of
Recurrent human drama.
Evil and Deceit enfold and submerge
Now and then the life of righteousness.
Triumph righteousness will once again
Wait and see this happen.

Chivalry, however, is not wholly dead. The lone voice of Vikarna from the Kaurava benches rises in protest. But that voice is stifled by the anger of Karna who orders Duschasana to: "disrobe Panchali to show the world / She is no royal Princess but a mere / Slave of Duryodhana.''

In that royal court of hundreds of warriors, Panchali suffers immitigable insult and infamy, for the courtiers are worse than "tall trees with painted figures" which the poet laments. As Duschasana starts to disrobe Panchali, she knows she must somehow defend herself — or else? But what defense? Where is succor to be found? In this moment of despair, she makes the supreme gesture of complete surrender to God. Her faith in His grace is absolute, her rejection of all earthly supports is final; she lifts both her hands from the portion of the robe still covering her and joins them in an act of obeisance; the child's trust in the Mother. In his introduction to his Tamil rendering of the *Gita*, while explaining the verse: "Abandon all dharmas, and take refuge in me alone. I will deliver thee from all sin and evil, do not grieve," Bharati says:

Sri Ramanujacharya taught that, while one is caught in this sea of *samsara*, one should surrender to the Divine with hands uplifted, just as the drowning person holds his hands above the water (that is, abandoning all movements of his hands). This self same truth is revealed also in the life of Panchali. It is only when she removed her hand from the robe that she was wearing, and lifted both hands above her head, that through the grace of the Lord Krishna her honor was saved and robes grew on her and tired the hands of Duschasana.

High above the fog of evil surrounding her, Panchali raises her voice in a mighty crescendo of prayer invoking the grace of Krishna:

> Thou sky within sky, thou element
> Of the elements, earth, air, water, fire;
> Thou who lightest the hearts
> Of sages in deep meditation;
> Thou that fondly holdest the hand
> Of your consort Lakshmi
> Whose dwelling is in the lotus
> That blooms in the forest pond!
> Thou the first of all beginnings,
> Shore and center of all knowledge,
> Thou light of all lights,
> Thou that ridest on Garuda
> Who soars high in the sky,
> Krishna, thou flame of truth,
> Thou rich immaculate grace,
> Hear me, save me.

This prayer, that seems to carry within it the sorrows endured by women through aeons past, is the brightest diamond in the drama, which is itself a galaxy of flashing gems. In the original, each word of the prayer happens to be the right word in the right place. "She cried, her voice swelled / Like the woes of liars, like woman's pity, / Like the flame of the wise, / Like the waves of the troubled sea." Her prayer is heard and she is saved. It is a miracle, but miracles do still happen. God *is* a reality whose Grace, a well of living waters, still sustains the Hindu way of life. As "tired Duschasana sank upon the floor,"

> The assembled kings raised the shout:
> Hail! all hail to Shakti!
> Only the snake-bannered Kuru
> Hung down his head in shame.

Bharati was a great believer in Shakti. Shakti worship was his forte. In this portrayal he brings to us all the poignancy of great wisdom and justice failing to avert evil for the lack of action. After this overwhelming scene, we have the "aftercourses." Panchali takes a terrible vow. In the words of K. R. Srinivasa Iyengar:

Alone, outraged beyond calculation, towering above the pigmy humanity that has conspired to humiliate and crush her, — her heart reviving in an ecstasy of gratitude, her eyes flashing pestilential fires — Panchali grows into a fearful goddess of revenge, and in a volcanic burst of resentment leaves her dishevelled abundant tresses ungathered, turns on her unmanly tormentors in a blaze of fury, and pronounces the ominous uncompromising vow that comprehends the total doom of the Kauravas.[19]

Bhima's vow is to destroy Duryodhana and Duschasana, Arjuna's to annihilate Karna. But Panchali's vow outsoars theirs in sheer ferocity:

> Not till the fiend Duschasana's blood
> Mingles with demon Duryodhana's
> And I smear my tresses with their blood
> And then bathe and wash it away —
> Not till then will I gather again
> These my tresses unloosened and wild!

After the final insult to womanhood, Panchali takes her uncompromising vow on behalf of oppressed womanhood. Bharati is no doubt forecasting a new chapter for Indian womanhood when every woman would become, not only a Mother, but Mother Might, the Power that is indispensable for the life of man on earth.

Bharati's *Panchali* is also a projection of India's political consciousness. Indeed, some find the whole verse drama an expression of Bharati's political protest. Thus Panchali is Mother India, while Duryodhana and his allies are the foreign forces of exploitation, and Bhishma is the mouthpiece of the moderates. One could carry this parallelism even further and find in Bhima a symbol of extremism and in Arjuna the sustained power of *satyagraha*. This verse drama was written midway between Bharati's earlier extremism and latter-day faith in Gandhi's nonviolence. Arjuna's words seem to summarize the Indian situation in 1918-19. "To-day we are bound, let's bear it with patience / Times must change, and dharma must triumph: / And Gandiva, my mighty bow is here."

One thing is certain. Panchali is the image of Mother India in shackles but still defiant, in the most critical moment of her ageless life. In his exile Bharati's one desire was to see India freed and restored to her original glory. The docile and cowed people of India excited his fury, and he chose this theme of the tragic consequences of unquestioning submission to ancient customs and conventions and of a fatalistic attitude to express it. The poet wanted an inquisitive people challenging by thought and action the subjugated condition of their existence. Bharati thought, no doubt, that Divine Grace alone could achieve the miracle of India's emancipation. Only when the extremists and moderates among India's politicians were silenced and the country surrendered to the soul force of *satyagraha* could the miracle of its emancipation come about. Seen thus, *Panchali Sapatham* was "a prophecy of freedom through the Gandhian movement."[20]

Panchali is an emanation of Mahashakti, the Power Creatrix, as well. There are moments in the history of the world when the resources and efforts of man are doomed to failure. Then Para Shakti becomes an active force on earth. Sri Aurobindo describes the saving of Truth on earth by Savitri's soul power. So have Maithili Saran Gupta's "Saket," "Panchavati," Dinkar's "Kurukshetra" and "Urvasi," Michael Madhusudan's "Megnadh Vadh Kavya," and Pukalendi's "Nala Venba." Bharati describes the immaculate power of Panchali that saves the Pandavas, and wins the battle of Dharma. Panchali's real nature as Shakti is emphasized throughout this drama. The dicing of Panchali moved Shakti in the heavens. While

Brahma, Vishnu, Siva, and Surya were petrified, it was Shakti who received a new lease of life: "Youthful Uma, Kali herself the Strong / The Original Shakti with her terrible bow, / The Supreme Knowledge that destroys Illusion, / Who saves by her smile while riding a lion." This Shakti is roused and descends into Panchali; now Victory is certain, for Parashakti enters into Panchali's being. The insulted and injured Queen, womanhood fighting for her due place in the world of men, Mother India struggling to be free, and Mahashakti in the plenitude of her splendor — these four attributes emerge in that immortal character turning from men to God in the center of the Kuru Court.

"Till *Panchali Sapatham*, the Tamils had no great dramatic literature."[21] In this poetic drama with its clash of towering personalities — a mixture of good, evil, sedate, and virile — Bharati has given to Tamil literature one of its greatest assets which abounds in poetic beauty and contains a splendid description of the downtrodden womanhood of India, humiliated yet undaunted.

V *Kuyil Pattu*

Kuyil Pattu is a narrative written as a dramatic monologue in the *ahaval* meter which corresponds to blank verse in English. This poem of 750 lines is a fable about an Indian nightingale or cuckoo, a bull, and a monkey. The human characters are a prince and a poet. The story came to the poet in a dream, a kind of vision of beauty and love.

Critics find *Kuyil Pattu* the "purest" poetry among Bharati's three major works. Some compare it to "Dante's *Divine Comedy* and hail it as the 'Epic of the Soul'."[22]

Kuyil Pattu begins with the vision of the cuckoo in the enchanted silence of the mango grove in Pondicherry, inspiring love at first sight which the poet feels and the bird expresses. The solitary cuckoo is surrounded by a few males of the species. The musical notes make the poet drowsy. And then, reality shades into the dream in which the bird laments the impermanence of love. Love-Death; joy-misery; harmony-discord; fame-shame — such are the antinomies with which the cuckoo fashions her music:

> Love, Oh love without end:
> And love failing,
> Death, but death for ever.
> Joy, unending joy:

> And joy failing,
> Misery, misery.
> Divine the poetic voice:
> But when rhythm fails,
> Mere confusion.

Bharati is drawn to the bird when her winged listeners fly away leaving her alone and sorrowing. He asks her the reason for her sad-sweet song. "I seek love — or death!" answers the cuckoo. At this stage Bharati raises our curiosity to its zenith in the supernatural world or, as some may say, in a fairy tale. The cuckoo disappears with its heartfelt request that the poet come there on the fourth day. The poet, too, is madly in love with the dark bird, and looks forward to the rendezvous.

Still in the power of the enchantment of the previous experience and driven by love's impatience the poet goes to the garden the very next day. He feels the eternal darkness enshroud him. He is overpowered as though haunted by twenty ghosts all at once. In the glorious light of the sun, the trees glisten. He moves like a puppet drawn by a thread to the scene of the previous day. To his horror, he finds the cuckoo shamelessly flirting with a gibbering, gesticulating monkey. The sword of the jealousy-stricken poet flashes forth to kill the monkey. But he restrains himself and listens to the love talk of the bird. The cuckoo gives a delightful account of the many merits of the monkey which are denied to man. Bharati has his own dig here at the antics of "civilized man":

> Should men with garments true to hide
> Their bodies lacking your silken hair
> And strut before your beauteous form:
> Should they their beard and moustache trim
> And preen to vie with your loved face:
> Should they in imitation drink and dance
> And scale with ladders temple tops:
> Still can they jump and leap like you?
> Where can they get a tail so fine?
> Will a tucked up garment do the trick,
> Or a trailing rag-like turban end?
> Yet, leaping, flying soaring high,
> What can match your tail divine?
> For brains and vegetarianism.
> No race to equal the monkey clan.

The poet's infatuation ultimately blinds him to the reality, and he flashes forth his sword, but both bird and beast vanish.

In the next scene, the poet returns home unconscious. When he comes to his senses in the evening he has no strength left to explain to his friends who are alarmed at his condition. He sleeps after partaking of the milk and food offered by the mother Goddess Shakti.

Unable to bear the suffering of darkness, he sings of the glories of the rising sun. He returns the next day to the garden only to find the bird now flirting audaciously with an old bull. Bharati bursts into an exclamation to the creator on the wonders of music. The vision disappears as soon as the sword from the hands of the jealous poet flashes forth at the bull.

The story grows more intriguing and mysterious, our curiosity is kindled. Suspense almost reaches the breaking point. The fourth day dawns and the poet is slowly dragged on by a speck of darkness, which becomes in time the cuckoo, to the old mango grove. He meets the bird and charges her with falsehood which he had himself seen. The mystery is still further heightened by the desperate cry of the cuckoo reaching its perfection in her absolute self-surrender to Fate, leaving it either to burn her away if discarded by the poet or to marry her to him if he accepts her.

What follows is a continuation of the same scene but with a narration by the sage of Podikai of the story of the cuckoo's previous birth. She is the daughter of Murugan, the hunter of the mountains. Out of pity she consents to marry her maternal uncle's son Madan (bull), but her parents agree to give her away in marriage to Kurangan (monkey) a son of Pulian (tiger) of wealth and heroism. But she goes to a grove where she is seen by the Prince of Vanchi and they fall in love with each other at first sight. While they are lost in bliss, Madan and Kurangan surprise them there. The two burn with rage at the sight of the lovers in embrace and their swords pierce through the back of the prince. The prince turns and kills them, but himself collapses, hopeful of meeting his beloved in his next birth. Murugan's daughter is next reborn as the cuckoo.

Another chapter, as it were, opens when a sage prophesies her meeting her lover the prince. The bird naturally asks him how a cuckoo can marry a human being. The sage reveals to her that she is herself a lady born and transformed into a bird by ghosts of the bull and the monkey who had somehow met her and who were even then anxious to have her avoid embracing once again the prince of her heart. The sage foretells that the ghosts will create the illusion of her

making love to the bull and the monkey so that the prince will accuse
her of falsehood and pretension when she meets him. The sage does
not conclude the story, but he says that she will know herself how the
whole story will end. Once again we are kept in suspense.

In the last part of the dream the poet's heart is moved, and he
realizes that the scenes of the previous two days were illusions. The
cuckoo's words clear the mists of misunderstanding, and the poet
ardently kisses the tiny bird now perched on his hand. And lo and
behold! the cuckoo vanishes. In her place there stands a maid angelic
and flawless, the very Spirit of Beauty:

> A maid stood there with radiant delight
> And eyes cast down; she looked at me and bowed.
> Lord, to limn her beauties in homely speech!
> The man-devouring wonder of her eyes!
> To seize the depths of meaning in her gaze!
> This is all I can say to the learned and wise;
> Mixing the juice of poesy and the essence of verse,
> Seasoning with nectar and congealing with love, —
> Even so Almighty fashioned this angel.

The poet's love has found its fruition. He kisses her wine-red lips in
gay abandon. But the rapture suddenly ends, and the poet wakes up
into the workaday world and realizes he is only in his own house; the
old book, the pen, the bundle of newspapers, and the old mat are all
in their usual place, far from the breezy grove and delectable
daydreams!

Here is a glimpse of the poet's house through just a few fugitive
flashes, but revealing in its classic restraint his home as no rank
realist poet would. The poverty of the old mat coming like the poison
and sting at the very end of the scorpion's tail is poignant in its very
nakedness of assertion, yet the poet is oblivious of its earthly
significance except as his old companion, his mother's lap, as it were,
sending him to rest and to sleep, the very symbol of Mother Nature
with her alternating rhythm of spreading-out evolution and the
rolling-up involution. There are the remaining three: first, the book
of old poetry — a perennial fountain in which he gets lost only to
gain his new inspiration, and which though as fresh as the morning
breeze yet is grown old in his hands by constant use; second, his pen
which reduces the elaboration of this inspiration to the choicest
words of sweet poetry; third, the newspapers — in which these poems
appear in print — which go forth as his message to the world and
which bring him back news of all the men and women of the world,

the alter egoes of his own Absolute self, perhaps enjoying the well-earned rest like himself in the isolation of their soul in the perfect equality of the really democratic world of sleep.

This dream is often described by critics as the "colossus of a dream taller than most."[23] It is really *samadhi*, the long and eternal dream which supervenes the ordinary waking consciousness. Aldous Huxley writes, "For most of us, most of the time, the world of everyday experience seems rather dim and drab. But for few people often, and for a fair number occasionally, some of the brightness of the visionary experience spills over, as it were into common seeing and the everyday universe is transfigured." It is this transfiguration which is referred to as the colossus of the dream and justifies taking this poem as a journey to the antipodes of the waking consciousness or as the spiritual experience of the mystic.

Only great poetry can lend itself to so many interpretations and still remain unexplained completely. It is possible to see some similarity between Bharati's fable and the Western story of Beauty and the Beast. The roles are reversed here; the poet accepts without reservation the cuckoo's love at last, the cuckoo ceases to be a bird, the spell is broken, and she regains her true self.

The setting of a lonely cuckoo singing of its disenchantment, perched invisibly on a bough in a darkling wood, recalls Shelley's image of "A widow bird sate mourning for her love / Upon a wintry bough." The cuckoo, beauty gentle and weak, is tested by fate. A frail insignificant thing, whose only claim to life is its melodious voice, is subjected to a cruel fate, for it cannot attain its love easily.

The cuckoo *is* love; and love is more easily aligned with sorrow than with joy, for love falls an easy prey to illusion. True love is hard to come by; and when such a true marriage of souls is effected, the resulting joy is akin to a divine union — hence its glory cannot survive the touch of the mundane. Therefore Beatrice is to be met only in Paradise; and the mortal kiss offered to the cuckoo by the poet only leaves him alone, with but a memory of the divine rapture. But this ambrosial memory is enough to redeem the mortal. This true love, then, is a mystic phenomenon, a vision of the eternal. "Oh tell me, the most learned amongst you, whether / you find any secret of the Vedas in my day dream?"

VI *Philosophical and Religious Poems*

While Bharati was a deeply religious man, he had no patience with obscurantism or the external trappings of the religious orders. He did not accept caste divisions and could separate with ease the grain and chaff in Hindu traditional beliefs. He believed in the "Wisdom and Spirit of the Universe" and in the embodied manifestations of that Power as Rama, Krishna, or Muruga. "Even in days of acute distress, he could enter into a prayerful mood and surrender to the will of God."[24]

Bharati's experiments in religious and philosophical free verse were attempted at various times and probably date from his earliest excursions into Vedic literature. Midway through his Pondicherry exile, he was turning into a Vedantin by temperament. His desire then was to express himself naturally, forcefully, yet effortlessly, with the least possible literary "craftsmanship."

In his religious and philosophical poems Bharati's creative spirit achieves an unimpeded flow. Wave after wave of feeling surges through them flowing with ripples and bubbles, while in some there are turbulent eddies and floods. Rooted in the *Vedas*, the lover of religion and philosophy in Bharati comes to the fore. His are indeed sustained lyrical outpourings in praise of God, the words radiant with the glow of joy. What if life was full of battle scars! The life of imagination was the poet's own, and had its own sovereignty.

The bulk of the religious poetry of Bharati consists of songs and hymns on the various Gods and Goddesses of the Hindu pantheon. "These poems are not however merely on the old and hackneyed pattern of the earlier Tamil poets. There is something new and modern, not only in the form but also in thought content of most of these songs."[25]

An invocation to the Sun starts "Heat is mother of light. . . . / Fire is the heroic God. / Fire is Sun." Then follow a few beautiful hymns to Agni (the Vedic God of Fire)

> Rain, Wind, Thunder
> Lightning Flashes.
> We praise lightning.
> May it light up our knowledge.
> The cloud children throw down lightning blossoms.
> There's no place sans electricity.
> Even so are all the gods.
> In black silicon, white sand, green leaf,
> Red flower, blue cloud,
> In air, sky — electricity is dormant everywhere.
> We praise that.

Bharati's prayer songs are extremely popular among South Indian musicians. He has sung on almost all Hindu deities. Inspired by the

Manakkula Vinayakar Temple in Pondicherry he composed a garland of forty verses to Ganesha. He was then an exile, and he could
see no silver lining in the threatening skies. But he is as defiant as
ever:

> No fear, no death by water:
> No shame, no body's trembling;
> No sin, no hiding;
> We shall nothing fear.
> Let the earth quake, yet fear not!
> Let the sea boil and rise, be not afraid!
> We shall fear none and nothing.
> Fear nor place nor time.
> The sky is here, and the monsoon too:
> The sun, wind and water.
> Fire, earth, the moon and stars:
> We have body, life and knowledge,
> Food for life and maids to love,
> Songs to hear, and the worlds to see
> And Ganapati's name to chant —
> Eternal these; poor heart,
> All hail, in goodness live.

Bharati's utter faith results in Tamil expression of surpassing
beauty, as in *"Muruga"* for example:

> In the temple of knowledge
> On the lap of Grace
> You rest with your lightning spear,
> Come, make new our life on earth.

Or as in "Nandalala": "With your touch Krishna, I thrill / When
my finger feels the flame." Again, in another poem:

> High above the worlds of our seeing
> You have reared the Temple of Bliss:
> And you have taught us too the way to scale it
> Leaning on Love Divine.

Fearlessness and love are Bharati's two medicines for all the ills of
life: "There is no penance more potent than Love / Those who love
are by nature filled with joy eternal." Bharati brings about the symbolism of religious myths. Here is his interpretation of the
Resurrection:

If Sense is nailed to the Cross of Truth
By Austerity,
Jesus of the strenghtened Soul
Will rise as the boundless sky.

Mary Magdalene is External Feminine
Jesus Christ is deathless Dharma,
Draw we close to the Symbol.
Look, an inner meaning flows.

At the heart of Bharati's religious lyrics is the group of Shakti
Songs. The deity enshrined in his heart was Shakti — the Mother
Might. It is the primordial power that makes and unmakes the whole
universe. In most of his literary creations, Mother Shakti is at the
center. She pervades *Kannan Pattu* and *Panchali Sapatham*. A
whole section on Shakti has the magnificent opening:

In the flood of Shakti the Sun is a bubble.
In the lake of Shakti the Sun is a blossom.
Shakti is all pervading, limitless, endless
It brings movement to immobility.

Bharati's approach is personal and approximates to the Mother-
child relationship. He views her as Lakshmi or Saraswati, Kali or
Durga, Valli or Kannamma. As a kitten can safely depend on the
mother cat, we can safely rely on the Mother's Grace to effect our
passage through life. She may manifest herself in diverse forms but
there is the same Shakti behind them all:

Some describe Thee as Nature.
Others see Thee in the elemental Five:
Some equate Thee with the primordial Force.
And some call Thee fire, wisdom, god.

O wondrous Mother mine,
"Aum" is all the homage
That we can offer to Thee:
Enlighten and Bless, Mother!

In "Self Surrender to Shakti," Bharati offers hand, eyes, ears,
tongue, shoulders, feet, heart, mind, thought — all of him — to the
service of the Mother. She could put to good use this wondrous
machine called man:

> Having tuned aright a stringed lute,
> Shall we cast it on a rubbish heap?
> Hearken, Mother Might. You've given me life,
> And lit this lamp of reason —
> A burden, this, to earth, unless
> My thoughts can be turned to deeds.
> Vouchsafe me this power of action
> To achieve my country's weal.

Bharati is indeed vouchsafed this grace; he feels the living presence of Shakti in him:

> She said: Serve Me and thrive
> And mind not the fruits of action;
> She has chased all sorrows away,
> And wedded me to Joy.

The grace of Shakti teaches man to love, even as his love for all beings on earth prompts the descent of Her grace. All the contradictions of earthly existence are resolved in Her, and the devotee himself is merged in Her. Bharati emphasizes this creative significance of the Mother. She is the savior who redeems with a smile:

> You are Joy, O Kali,
> You have entered me:
> Then without you, O Kali,
> How can I be?

Very rarely does Bharati refer to the destructive aspect of Shakti. He no doubt realized that creation and destruction are but the reverse and obverse of the truth and of the universe. The seed dies to give birth to the plant. Our life is a marvel of daily renewal. But Bharati preferred to hymn the glories of the Savior rather than of the Destroyer. "Oozhi-k-koothu" (The Dance in the Final Destruction) is the most audaciously frenzied and most poetically articulate piece in the Bharati canon. When the universe cracks into the final rythmic rubble, the Mother Shakti dances amidst devastation and death to the tune of all the ravaging forces of Nature. The poet rejoices at the invitation of Shakti to witness this dance. The five elements resolve and merge in Shakti, and all mind, all thought melt away. All are in ruin and the destructive forces roam and roar aloud. There is nothing but the void and the madly dancing Shakti. All the forces dash and clash, creating a terrible, breathtaking rhythm. Kali's eyes flash with sparks that reach to the ends of the universe. It is the doomed hour, the reign of annihilation. Time perishes; the worlds perish and disappear. The great silence of Lord Siva prevails and sheds luster. Mother Shakti's divine frenzy is at last arrested by the advent of Siva in his auspicious form, and She caresses the hands of Her Lord, Siva. As terrible as Swami Vivekananda's "Kali the Mother," this poem is a powerful evocation of the Mother's dreadful aspect. She leaps into action, the demon hordes dance to the accompaniment of Gangali, and we see and hear the blood dripping:

> As the worlds mightily clash
> And crash in resounding thunder
> As blood dripping demon spirits
> Sing in glee amid the general ruin,
> To the beat and the tune
> Leapest thou, Mother, in dance ecstatic
> Dread Mahakali!
> Chamundi! Gangali!
> Mother, Mother,
> Thou hast drawn me
> To see the dance! . . .
> When the demon-hosts clash
> Hitting head against head,
> When the knocking and breaking
> Beat rhythmic time,
> When the sparks from your eyes
> Reach the ends of the earth,
> Then is the doomed hour
> Of Universal death!
> When Time and the three worlds
> Have been cast in a ruinous heap,
> When the frenzy has ceased
> And a lone splendor has wakened,
> Then Auspicious Siva appears
> To quench thy terrible thirst.
> Now thou smilest and treadst with him
> The blissful Drama of Life!

The chronic poverty at home was one of the external causes that drove Bharati to cultivate the self within. But his constant companionship with the *Upanishads* and the *Bhagavad Gita* had their effect. Swami Vivekananda was one of his favourite authors and Sri

Aurobindo's friendship whilst at Pondicherry helped him in assiduously tilling the inner fields of thought. His poetry became a kind of yoga, an effort to reach Illumination through the clouds of delusion.

> You thought of despoiling me
> O delusion!
> It is certain I shall annihilate you,
> O delusion!
> To one who is ready to die
> The ocean is not far off;
> They who realize this body's lie,
> What can you do to them, Delusion?

Death itself dies in the face of truth's glory. The perception of Truth is made possible by knowledge alone. The same poet who sings soulfully of gods and godheads also knows that ultimately these are but manifestations of one eternal truth:

> Listen! Can't you hear the Vedas say
> Knowledge is God?
> Would you lose and slay yourself
> In countless false religions?

Bharati's philosophical poems pose the tantalizing questions of I and You; truth and falsity; belief and agnosticism. He realizes the great good that devotion brings to one. He constantly struggles to control the wayward mind, lest it obstruct the path to self-realization. His soul first pauses at the problem of death and the means to achieve victory over it:

> Jesus died pinned to the Cross:
> Krishna by a swift arrow;
> Even Rama yielded to death by water:
> But I shall not die, 'tis certain.

He would root out lust and anger, the causes of death and realize the divine in everything. Yes, even in the pen and the sword, God resides unseen! His unfinished spiritual autobiography is "rooted in utter realism and bears mute witness to the tremendous loss sustained by Tamil literature in Bharati's premature end."[26] Out of the 6000 verses planned by him, only 66 are here, and they end with a declaration:

I shall give you the word
At the heart of all world faiths:
You are God; You are God; You are the Lord.
Thou Art That.
It is the blanket of ignorance
That says you are not this earth's God.
You are God; Remove that Ignorant veil,
And say "I am Siva" ever and always.

His religious and philosophical verse opened new vistas and tried new techniques in Tamil poetry.

CHAPTER 4

Bharati and the Indian Heritage

THE term heritage has been much diluted in meaning through its casual and miscellaneous use. Strictly speaking, it is a cumulation through the ages of a recurring phenomenon in the societal life of people of ancient stock who, through various historical changes, cling tenaciously to a sense of their own identity and continuity. Heritage is thus akin to an undying residuum of thought and experience which is periodically renovated or significantly extended with each momentous rebirth in the lives of such ethnic groups of people.

In this view there is no common European heritage. The Greek heritage was the product of non-Hellenic stocks. The Roman heritage was the work neither of Latins or Romans as such but of an ethnic mixture which was given a semblance of external uniformity by the Catholic church. Heritage in Western Europe is plainly not by birth but by gift. Not so in India. The Vedic past is still at the doors of the subcontinent; the epics and puranas are still the mental and spiritual pabulum of the masses. While the death of Sanskrit in every generation has been unflinchingly announced, its priceless treasures still function as the matrix of thoughts and feelings, hopes and visions of the teeming population of India. Thanks to this historical fact, Indians have always striven to be themselves in fundamentals.

Secondly, the term heritage has come to be restricted to a consideration of cultural activities to the exclusion of all those urges which alone furnish the key to an understanding or appraisal of them. It is significant to note that in the West the Reformation followed the Renaissance while in India it has been almost always a simultaneous or parallel development. Indians as a rule label everything religious in order to achieve a total and integral view of man, nature, and the universe. Hence their art and morality, reason and intuition, science and philosophy seem, to the uninitiated, a fantastic jumble of heterogeneous or disparate entities. Much that passes under the religious label in India is literature in the Western sense, while what passes for literature in India is invariably sustained by a religious or mystic significance. Indian lyrics like those of her saints give an abiding religious appeal, while her great religious scripture — the *Gita* — is a song as its title claims. This two-way passage between the seen and the unseen, the past and present, the here and hereafter, is so intricately woven into the texture of Indian consciousness that the dividing line between them has vanished utterly.

In the chronological view, the first phase of India's resurgence in modern times was on the religious plane. The founder of the Arya Samaj, Dayanand Saraswati, was ignorant of English, but he met the challenge of the modern world of Western science and liberal thought and held his ground. Its Bengal variant which preceded it was also first more theological than literary; but both assumed a political complexion under the stress of prevailing conditions. The literature that they gave rise to was primarily one of revolt against the West in general and England in particular, and it represented a return to the sanctuaries of India's own past.

It is against this background that we should view the life and labors of Subramanya Bharati. He was one of the self-taught men of genius of whom India has had as good a share as other great cultures; for he imbibed the wisdom of the race along with the air he breathed, and he proved a precocious prodigy as well. A brief stay in Benares during the most impressionable years of his life helped him to feel the pulse of India's life beneath her outward quiescence and pointed to him the way he was to go. The rough and tumble of revolutionary politics made a firebrand of him, and a decade of exile at Pondicherry enabled him to dedicate himself to the muse. They were years of extraordinary personal strain but equally extraordinary creative effort. When he returned to Madras and tried to pick up the broken threads of his life, frustration and failing health hastened him to an early grave.

Bharati appeared in an age of democracy and his successful utilization of the prevailing rhythm of colloquial Tamilian speech helped to change the very idiom of Tamil poetry, thereby giving a respectability to the language of the common man which henceforth became the standard language of Tamil poetry.

Surely a poet forms part of the glorious and continuous generation of cultural leaders who form a fraternity of light and love, representing a unity of culture and civilization, of philosophy and history. In this sense, Bharati represents the rich heritage of the perennial culture of his land. Indian culture may be looked upon as an ancient tree with branches of varying shapes full of flowers of different colors and fragrance, though all these branches depend on and draw nourishment from, the roots. There is in Bharati the heritage of the branch and also the heritage of the trunk and the roots. The common Indian culture represents the latter, whereas its special branch can be spoken of as the Tamilian heritage. Bharati is an Indian nationalist as well as a Tamilian. To him Tamil and India are but two aspects of one great truth of his heart. Thus he sings of them both in one of his songs, where he starts speaking of the Tamilians and ends in widening the sphere of reference till he speaks of them all as one whole country:

> Long Live Tamil
> Long Live Tamilians
> Long Live India.

He does not feel any difference between the Dravidians and the Aryans.

Though he speaks of the "New India" the "New Tamilians" and the "New women of India," he is not breaking away from the glories of India's historical past. From one point of view, the revolution he prays for is the reestablishment of the ancient glories of India. His complaint against the Indian enemies of freedom is that they are not true to the genius of India and its culture. Therefore, his nationalism is unlike much modern-day nationalism; it is something spiritual and cultural to him. India is to Bharati a symbol of a culture which immediately reminds him of his father, mother, and the continuous line of ancestors who lived and died, developing this great culture in a thousand and one ways. These names are incantations which bring back to his mind the infancy of his cultural ancestors, both men and women, who played, sang, and danced in his motherland, making their children immortal in the world of thought through the milk they fed them on, raising temples and ideals, growing ever heavenward, and making the very dust and waters pregnant with meaning, reminiscent of old history and glory. This is Bharati's India; full of wisdom, full of peace of mind, full of self-sacrifice, full of learning, full of music, poetry, dance, heroism, learning, and goodness. It is not that he is blind to the geographical unity but to him that is the outward reflection of the transcendental beauty, love and glory of the spiritual culture. The beauties of Nature, the ambrosia of rivers, the divine zephyr, the heaven-reaching Himalayas, the mother cow and the cooperative ox ploughing the land all have a historical, cultural, moral, and spiritual significance for Bharati in addition to their aesthetic beauty. Bharati reminds us so often of the past history of India's glorious culture. He makes us see India and her culture stand for truth, for equality, and for the great message of her sacred books, which are all the real wealth of any nation or culture. India is great because, in spite of the vicissitudes of history, she has kept her flag of culture high aloft. The freedom, which the poet wished for India, is for the perpetuation and development of this culture. He himself states that India demands freedom in order to give a new message of truth to the world. In this nationalism becomes true inter-nationalism. "Indian heritage" beginning with the *Vedas,* which spoke of the "whole world as one family is thus preserved in the poetry of Bharati."[1]

But the evolution of Bharati's genius and craftsmanship is remarkable for its consistent expansiveness and comprehensiveness. The popular adoration of him as the poet of patriotism is the least of his claims to enduring fame. But even so, the higher implications of his patriotic fervor are not so widely realized as they should be. To put it briefly, patriotism is not simply a secular motif with Bharati. When he thinks of the suffering of the ostracized Lala Lajpat Rai, he dreams of that leader, thinking of India in a distant land, in terms of the glorious heroes of the past, Arjuna, Karna, and the great Sikh Gurus. In that way his revolution is not a real revolution, but only an attempt at removing the unhealthy excrescences which in the Middle Ages had grown so huge and strong as to prevent the free flow of the perennial stream of Indian culture.

It would be more correct to call Bharati's patriotism as "matriotism" or even "matriolatry." For the worship of the mother elevated above the temporal sense becomes the worship of the supreme Shakti to which all creation is a kind of divine play. She is one in three and three in one, and she is the personalized or con-cretized expression of the Vedantic absolute. Sri Lakshmi is the winsome, ever youthful maiden dreamed of by poets, Saraswati is Uranis or the embodiment of wisdom, while Durga or Kali is the terrible one who destroys in order to usher in new creation. In his "Tintern Abbey" Wordsworth gives us a similar vision of three in one which leads him to equate the spirit of nature with the wisdom and spirit of the universe. Says Bharati:

In my youthful vision I saw a maiden fair, seated on a lotus throne, guitar in hand. I was enthralled by those ravishing strains wafted with the southern breeze. She stirred my halting muse to utterance with a light smile. She played hide and seek with me, leaving me forlorn by day and sleepless by night. In wild untrodden ways, in dark and silent mountain-pools through rustic homes, in high mansions and high populous cities, I sought her, in vain. And then one dark night, an awesome figure divinely fair, virgin-pure, came to me with outstretched arms. With the fire of longing I approached her. But lo! it was the mother indeed — the Parashakti whose grace is what we need first and last.

These are the "Three Loves" whom he has celebrated in a triptych. He thus loaded a political emotion with a metaphysical significance which goes deep into our subliminal consciousness.

Even when he speaks of the freedom of women, he reminds us of the great women of the past, all representing the varied aspects of the one divine force of love and motherhood, the great Shakti with whom he identifies his motherland. Similarly, the Tamil language reminds him of the spiritual heights reached by Kamban, Ilango, and Thiruvalluvar, of the heroism of the Pandyas and Cholas, and the glories of all the great leaders of Tamilnadu. Tamilnadu was to Bharati a land of sweetness, fame, and knowledge.

His religion is not different from this universal culture of transcendental truth immanent everywhere in India, in her culture and in her physical realities. He speaks of many godheads of this land — Ganapati, Siva, Krishna, Subrahmanya, Kali, Durga, Saraswati, Lakshmi, of Allah, of Christ — but they are the various poetic and spiritual ways of looking at one and the same great transcendental divine reality, ultimately experienced in the activities of this subcontinent, which again reflect "the rich Indian heritage, preached by poets and saints from the days of Vedas down to the modern times of Ramalinga and Ramakrishna."[2]

Bharati was essentially a lyric poet; but in the Indian tradition there is a genre which blends the lyric in an unique fashion with the epic and the dramatic into an organic whole. His best dramatic improvizations on a lyrical base in this genre are elaborately worked out in what are known as the Kannan songs. They are redolent of Indian classical memories derived from the epics, the puranas, and folklore. The Greek pantheon has found a wider and more hospitable home in the West; but its beauty and splendor are also felt by Indians since they have an analogue to each one of them, often improved for home use. Pleasure, edification, piety, and unction are harmoniously exercised on an intensely human and familiar level. It is a dictum of the Indian classical tradition that there can be nothing new in art functionally speaking, and that art's only justification is to exercise the primary feelings with all the artist's possible resources of invention and nuances of style. It is, therefore, the pleasures of recollection, the joy of rediscovery that justify Indian poetry. The descent from above and the ascent from below that meet halfway in Indian art are so aptly reflected in Bharati and together offer a glimpse of the timeless in the temporal.

The classical stimulus to Bharati's lyrical impulse is seen somewhat differently at work in his masterly epitome of the *Mahabharata* in *Panchali Sapatham*. The epic is the predominant note here; but the supremely dramatic scenes are interspersed with lyrical outpourings. By the same token his *Kuyil Pattu* carries the hallmark of a born lyricist, using common, almost threadbare unconsidered material.

Bharati has also contributed to the vers libre of modern times though he does not call it free verse. We can easily see the true nature of such compositions of his. These are not to be sung like other poems of his but to be recited. They have parallel construction; they remind us of the *Vedas* thus offering another example of preserving through an original creation the most ancient vedic literary form in modern Tamil.

Even when expressing the most revolutionary ideas, Bharati has at the back of his mind the message of one or the other great Indian poet or sage. In describing the principle of democracy, he explains it "on the basis of the old song of Avvai learnt by every Tamil child going to school."[3]

> There is no caste except two
> Those who are great and munificent and
> Those who are mean and selfish.

Here is a moral and spiritual democracy of love and service of all human beings forming a fraternity of God's children. This democracy believes in perfect equality because every man embodies God in himself. The individual is therefore as important and as divine as the society. One cannot exist without the other. Therefore, there is no place in this democracy for exploitation or slavery. Man has to be free from animal wants if he is to progress heavenwards to perfection. The society, if it is worthy of its name, should provide for the individual's minimum physical necessities and animal comforts. The world that fails to discharge this primary duty and hence tolerates suffering caused from hunger and the individual's consequent degeneration to the subhuman level has to be destroyed, to be rebuilt according to the true principles of divine democracy. It is this ideal society that Bharati cherishes. "If there will be no food for even a single individual let us destroy that world," sings Bharati. This is no material communism, but the gospel of the divinity of the individual. The poem has to be read as a whole and then it will be seen how it preserves the Indian heritage so beautifully summarized in Thirukural: "If one has to live by begging alone, let the creator of that social world vanish in thin air."

Even when Bharati praises the new spirit of freedom in other coun- tries, fighting against force and tyranny, he describes that spirit, true to the Indian literary heritage. In praising Belgium for courageously fighting Germany in World War I, he has in mind, though not specifically stating it, the war of righteousness against the demons, where the victory for the time being may be on the wrong side. He mentions the simile of the sacrifice and also the simile of the lamp light. Sacrifice is not defeat; for success is reaped a thousandfold after a while. The lamp may fail but the day is sure to dawn. The poet remembers the heroism of the mountain lasses of Nilgiris who without anything more than a sieve in their hands, tried to protect their lands, their children, and others with their makeshift shields. After all, heroism is an attitude of the mind and does not consist in the choice of weapons. Again, in describing Russia, he speaks of the dance of Kali and compares the fall of the Czar to the fall of the Himalayas. In that poem he uses proverbs and onomatopoeia, bring- ing out the richness of the colloquial rhythm of Tamil.

In his more permanent prose works, Bharati develops the folk songs as their source which have a continuous history in Tamilnadu from the Sangam age. Bharati has, as nobody else had before him, discredited the vogue of "poetic diction" and dealt with themes close to modern life against the background of the Indian heritage. Not that he was a conservative in temper or outlook. He was traditional, if at all, only in going to the bedrock for his emotional and spiritual sustenance. He believed it possible and necessary to reconcile the old with the new, and he showed the way to do so as well. "If Tamil has attained a new dignity, a new expressiveness and suppleness, it is wholly due to the labors of Bharati."[4] All his writings are true to the heritage of India; these show all that is eternal and still living in this heritage and how it continues to be significant even in the nuclear age.

CHAPTER 5

Patriotic Writings

WHAT relation there should be between poets and national movements has been the most crucial literary problem of our century. A poet is a mirror which reflects the rise, development, progress, renaissance, degradation, and downfall of a country. It is only through their poetic genius that writers such as Homer, Dante, Shakespeare, Milton, Vyasa, and Valmiki have obtained immortality. Further, each one of them had used their talents in commemorating an outstanding period of their lifetime. Truly, poets are the live nerves of a country who electrify others by their forceful words. In Bharati there is a steady, ceaseless and burning desire to shake off the yoke of an alien rule which finds immortal expression in his soul-stirring national songs. Carping critics of Bharati have charged him with "trying at times too deliberately to be political, and writing verse more political than poetical."[1] Some of this criticism may have been captious, but the risk is a real one in Bharati. Even in some poems of high quality may be felt a certain faltering at the close, when he seems to try to resolve his discords without quite finding the right key.

Bharati has been saved from becoming merely, or too facilely, a political poet like so many others by a strong inner resistance, a matter of both temperament and conviction. All imaginative poets and writers are conscious of divided minds, opposing intuitions, and this is true of Bharati more than of most. Critics have noticed how often in his earlier and middle work his poems turn on a kind of duality, as if he were struggling to reconcile two contradictory visions of life. He was himself an odd mixture, one is tempted to say, of indolence and energy; he appeared to possess both inclination to contemplate existence through an opium pill and a compulsion to act. To get Bharati to answer a letter was nearly as vain as any human endeavor can be; the "violent hatred of letter writing" that Coleridge found in

Wordsworth was at least as strong in Bharati. Yet the spirit of the age drew him along a path necessarily toilsome, at times perilous.

Poets everywhere in our chaotic age have faced conflicting claims — each right in its own way — of old and new, present and future, Utopia and possibility, emotion and reason, worker and intellectual, individual and society. Perhaps by now we have seen enough to conclude that the poet's true function is not to identify himself too closely with one demand or the other, but to mediate or hold the balance between them. And perhaps it is in this direction that instinct and experience guided Bharati. Some of his fellow poets, in the subcontinent as elsewhere, had withdrawn into ivory towers; some had made themselves mouthpieces of political leaders; some had stopped writing. Bharati's inner conflicts, painful as they may have been, were a symptom of health rather than of weakness, of a civic spirit combined with an artistic sense too strong to let him be swamped by the tidal force of the national movement. Like all great and heroic movements the Indian independence movement has been apt to reduce individual men and women to units in its army, ciphers in its great account, to its own cost as well theirs. The individual becomes nothing, the cause everything. Accident has helped to save Bharati from being submerged; the exile in Pondicherry, which had thrown him most of the time on his own slender resources, really came as a blessing.

Bharati was born a quarter of a century after 1857, the year which saw India's first spontaneous revolt against British domination. No longer did the Indians believe in the British Empire as a divine boon. Various movements had started all over the country, waking the masses to consciousness of their thraldom. When Bharati came of age, the atmosphere was charged with slogans hailing, "My country, my religion, my language!" Poets and thinkers in India were expressing their burning nationalism through historical poems and essays, and most of them sang undiluted praise of the glorious past. All this left a deep impression on his formative mind. By nature, Bharati had been endowed with a keen intelligence, fortitude, strong will, and bubbling patriotism. He was pained and shocked at Indians' forgetting their own noble heritage and instead adapting themselves to English civilization, collecting English college degrees and high positions under alien rule. The call of national leaders like Lokmanya Tilak, Lajpat Rai, and Bepinchandra Pal kindled him to action. He, too, raised his voice to end slavery at any cost, expressing his anguish in his poetry:

Just as the sun rises, did not once
The sun of our glory rise high? Tell.
But He went from here to enjoy the West,
The dark night of decline came to trouble us.
O creepers! Are these lovely flowers nothing to us?
O birds! Your songs may be sweet but what are they to us?
We have no eyes to see because of slavery
We have no ears to hear because of slavery.

He goes on, in this long poem, in this strain and concludes the poem
thus:

O God! When will this dark night of slavery be over
When will the bright sun of Freedom dawn again?
When shall we get out of this cage, O God,
When shall our nation reach its nationhood again?

The poetry that flowed from the depths of his heart really aroused
Tamilnadu. It whipped the people into action. His words, "No fears!
No fears! / Fear there is none." inspired courage in his countrymen
who had been encircled in fear. On another occasion he burst out,
"When shall this thirst for liberty be quenched? / When will this
glamor for thraldom die?" It was natural that Bharati, "conscious of
India's spiritual wealth and profoundly convinced of its importance
to his countrymen would express himself in forms congenial to the
Indian spirit."[2] He wished to see India free to fashion for herself
these forms and chafed at anything which savored of the imposition
of alien customs of the West. He wrote:

Think not of India as of a child's buffoonery or a jester's
tricks and airs;
Here have sprung mighty heroes of faith, at whom the
world trembles.
Here have sprung sages that were lords of yoga, whose
light abides unto this day,
Men whose faith was their very life, their all, and the
world their home.
Yes, even here such kingly saints were born, and in the
hearts of all men they shone resplendent.
What boots it to bring here a masquerade of strange
disguises and of foreign airs?
All that you gain you'll squander in the end, and about
your neck ignominy shall lay her garland.

Another significant poem extols the virtues of village life and its simplicity. It underlines the importance of contentment with one's lot and warns against the temptations of the glamorous West. Some lines are given below:

> No beautiful palaces these,
> Only simple huts.
> There are diseases in palaces,
> How can disease dwell in a hut?
>
> Disease is a snob
> It loves to lie on cushions
> How can it survive
> on a rough mat in a hut? . . .
>
> In that small village in huts,
> Good farmers live
> They work hard on farms
> Lead straight and simple lives.
>
> Had I a thatched hut in such a place
> I would not have been poverty stricken,
> I would not have been dubbed less educated
> I would not have bothered about fame . . .
>
> Fame is just a feather
> which reaches people's heads
> After the bird has faced cartridges
> And that feather would also fall, one day!
>
> If a guest came from a distant land
> I get wonder struck to hear his tales
> "Is this world so big and wide,
> Are there such luxuries and shows?"
>
> I tell them in wonderment,
> I never compare my lot with the world's
> Does the Earth stop its movement
> Pining for the riches in Heaven?

The poem has the charm of "The Deserted Village" and the simplicity of "Prelude" and a high seriousness of its own. In a way this was the beginning of what was seen later in Gandhi's call of "Back to the Village," and which was so well expressed in Tagore's

"Matir dak." Bharati was searching for a nest, which would have given him spiritual satisfaction and solace from the pressures of urbanization and the breakdown of feudalism and colonialism. Such poems of social rebellion reveal the basic desire in the poet's mind to see the nation advance in all fields. Credit should be given to him that he did not fall prey to obscurantism or chauvinism.

In most of his patriotic poems he sings of Mother India. Bowing to her he says:

> Hail mother, we must say; we will certainly
> bow to this mother of this great land.
> Is it mean or shameful to bow to our most beloved
> Motherland?
> Even if you will tear my flesh into pieces,
> your will shall not be done,
> my breath will it stop?

Another of his popular poems begins with the lines:

> When as I heard men slander thee,
> Mother it grieved me so,
> For very rage I thought my soul would
> burst her bars and go!

It is part of the Indian tradition to bow to India and hail her as mother. Love of motherland was Bharati's electric light and faith in her emancipation was his switch. In all of his national songs one can see true depictions of heroism and lines capable of transforming sluggards into heroes. But at times, seeing the deplorable downfall of his fellow countrymen, he doubted within himself whether they would progress at all.

When the national struggle was at its height, Bharati's patriotic songs used to be sung in every lane of Tamilnadu with great fervor and feeling. "There was not a single public meeting or a single procession in which his songs 'Long Live Oh Mahatma,' 'Vande Mataram,' 'See the jewelled flag of our motherland,' were not sung."[3]

But Bharati did not stop merely with writing poetry. He put up a strong fight against foreign rule. In those days the reward for such a fight was either prison life or exile. If one were known to be patriotic, he was pounced upon, baton charged, bulleted, and his property confiscated. Bharati fought injustice, embraced poverty, stayed in exile at Pondicherry, and held out challenges containing fiery patriotic sentiments befitting every occasion. Even after his exile at Pondicherry, the undaunted Bharati with an upright head, majestic gait, and clear conscience attacked foreign rule vehemently. His ebullition of anger at his country reeling under foreign yoke, like the hiss of a snake, was proverbial. His was righteous indignation.

Day by day his love for free India increased. Indeed, while there was nothing exclusive in his patriotism, he could never understand how any conscientious Indian could be anything other than a fervent lover of his country. He was totally free from racial prejudice; his vision of a universal brotherhood of love was always his primary inspiration; but this in no way conflicted with his intense and particular love for the land of his birth.

Bharati shows himself as a prophet of the age in his essay "The Coming Age" wherein he anticipates the ideology behind land reforms in India. In it he declares that "for the West as well as the East, there is only one decent way of living, viz, to make the earth common property and live on it as fellow workers and co-partners." This was written in 1918. It is of interest here to note that in his essay "Wealth" Bharati specially mentions and unequivocally rejects the Communist way of solving the land problem adopted by Lenin as "the way of bloodshed and murder which India cannot follow," and suggests voluntary redistribution of lands in the same way as Vinobha Bhave now seeks to do. Bharati goes one step further and suggests that these land-gift meetings should be held before the local temple and that documents of redistribution should be cut in copper plates and added to temple records.

When he is in the mood, Bharati is capable of much sly humor. In "Some Political Maxims," he says: "Keep many spies and pay them well, but never believe in what they say, except when they warn you against your friends and counsellors." Another is a dig at the British: "Make fine promises with proper saving clauses, but withhold threats."

Bharati was one of the few patriots of his times who thought of national integration more than half a century ago. He often used to pose and answer questions himself on the subject in his writings. What is a nation? How can it be integrated emotionally? What equipment is needed? Where should we begin? What are its gradations? Or should the miracle be worked all at once? Should we envisage pitfalls and perils? How are we to safeguard against them? And more and more queries, ad infinitum and ad nauseam.

In his "clarion call to the nation" Bharati sings "Full three hundred million all shall live together, / or die, if so we must, well knit together." and in his varied writings on the subject of national integration, Bharati's "blue print is quite practical and worth examining."[4] Excerpts on his writing arranged subjectwise relate to common frontiers, common inheritance, common culture, common savior, common flag, common endeavor, common hope, and common destiny.

I   Common Frontiers

In order that all three hundred million people of India may realize their oneness, they should all bear in mind that they are all children of one common mother, Mother India. India is a great land, with well-defined frontiers. The silvery peaks of snow-packed Himalayas hem her to the North; the tapering beak of the sandy promontory where at the point of the holy tryst of three thundering seas the virgin Goddess is still engaged in wrapt meditation limits her to the South; and the East and West are protected by the waters of the Bay of Bengal and the Arabian Sea. He urged Indians to look upon this as the land of their birth with a two-eyed view and a totality of vision. This was Bharati's first step to National Integration.

II   Common Inheritance

Time and again Bharati reminded his countrymen of their great and common inheritance. He often recalled with pride the sacred lore of the hoary *Vedas* and the *Upanishads*, the spotless heroism of Rama, the ever-green gospel of the *Gita*, the philosophical dispassionateness of Janaka, the matchless archery of Arjuna, the renunciation of Bhishma, the unfailing munificence of Karna, the nonviolence of Buddha, the monism of Sankara, the poetry of Kalidas, and the unique valor of Sakuntala's son Bharata. He urged his people to cherish them since he was sure that this priceless heritage handed down to Indians from generation to generation would bind them together with hoops of steel.

III   Common Culture

"For over a thousand years and more," says Bharati, "our forebears have lived and died in the selfsame soil, whose sacred rivers their hoary bones enshrine." These ancestors of his countrymen have bequeathed unto them a rarified and unique culture, which even today commands the veneration of the world. And for "generation after generation our mothers have lighted the lamps of love, matrimony and progeny which are still kept burning, fed by the oil of purity, chastity and family affection. Many a tall temple did our fathers build to implant in us heaven-pointing ideals of plain living and high thinking. Long pilgrimages from one corner of the country to another, baths of ablution in far flung rivers, self denying paths of knowledge, of worship (Jnana Marga and Bhakti Marga) and the discharge of duty, with no eye for reward have all been bequeathed to us as part of their immaculate culture." Love of learning and the practice of compassion and the silent heroism of uncomplaining suffering are also the legacy of his countrymen. The patterns of India's music and systems of philosophy common to all parts of the subcontinent are also gifts of India's ancient culture. "With such a culture to warm our hearts, how could we be sundered, how brook disintegration?" asks the poet.

IV *Common Savior*

Bharati minces no words in reminding his countrymen of the strange irony of fate that caused the people of India to live in subjection and slavery under foreigners who divided them only in order to rule. It was then, according to the poet, that the vicious process of disintegration began to set in. But before its virus could vitiate the whole community, merciful heaven sent down a great leader (Mahatma Gandhi), who has since become the savior. He predicted that disruption will be stemmed and disintegration halted under Gandhi's leadership, and every village and hamlet in the whole length and breadth of the country will resound with jubilant cries of salutation to the land and victory to Gandhi. These thoughts are an echo of his famous song "Long Live Oh Mahatma."

V *Common Freedom*

The poet envisaged the coming of a universal freedom to India. It would sweep away the curses of centuries and blaze a new trail. There would be no highborn or lowborn, no prince or peasant, no blue blood or red, no sovereign or subject — all shall be kings of the country. In the light of that heaven-born freedom, each and every Indian would have the same equality of opportunity, each of the same value, weight, and price. In some of his editorials, he even made allowances for those Indians who had earlier opposed freedom and urged that they be given seats of honor at the sharer's feet. "If this fact is kept steadily in view," argued the poet, "national integration will become a reality and cease to be a fantasy."

VI *Common Flag*

In the common national flag, Bharati saw a symbol of Indian culture and philosophy, transcending all banners and insignias. The flag to him was symbolic of the honor of each and every denizen of the land. He wanted all to have a close look at it and lower their heads in cheerful adoration. And round the mast he saw a variegated crowd of doughty heroes, dedicated to the single purpose of keeping it flying. Among them Bharati visualized toughened Tamils, awe-inspiring Andhras, courageous Canarese, obdurate Oriyas, militant Marathas, resolute Rajputs, powerful Punjabis, and brave Bengalis — all keeping an endless vigil, the real price of liberty. "Can this be borne in mind and people not feel at one?" he questions.

VII *Common Endeavor*

Bharati wanted all his countrymen to work together and pool their resources in common for the enrichment and glorification of an overall national prosperity. He wanted engineers to divert the surplus waters of the Ganga and fertilize the barren wastes of Central India. He desired that large loads of yellow wheat from the Gangetic Delta be daily exchanged for the silky betel leaf of the Cauvery basin, and the tough tusks of milk-white ivory from the colourful Kerala be awarded as fitting rewards to the bards of mighty Maratha valor. He heard the profound orations of the oracles of Benares relaying through the streets of Kanchi, by means of a special broadcast. For the heroic exploits of the legendary Rajasthan he wanted to give as a reward the rich golden ore from the mines of Mysore. He envisaged merchants attracted from all over India to the pearl fishery of the extreme South. And not only this; he had in mind relaxation and merrymaking as well. "When all of us have thus applied our shoulders to the wheel, let us relax all together, paddling our light little canoes, along the moon-washed waters of northern rivers, to the enduring music of Telugu language, sung by the silver-tongued girls of golden Kerala." Bharati believed that when people of the subcontinent are engaged in such common endeavor and common barter, no power on earth can estrange them from one another.

VIII *Common Hope*

This bard of Tamilnadu had mighty hopes awaiting fulfillment. He viewed with his mind's eye his countrymen parading over the beetling heights of snow-clad Himalayas and Indian oceanliners ranging over all the Western seas. He thought of throwing a bridge over the gulf that cuts the Indian mainland off from Sri Lanka and of digging mines and wells deep into the entrails of earth to heave forth mineral and oil wealth. He envisaged all kinds of industries to be started by Indians that would manufacture and export all sorts of goods from pin and paper to powerful battleships. He wanted Indians to devise their own means to span the star-spangled sky and measure the world of the wondrous moon. "If such hopes are shared by every Indian breast," says Bharati, "who can bar our forward leap to progress?"

IX *Common Destiny*

Thus the poet brought about a unity and uniformity of being and becoming, deep beneath all this seeming diversity. He visualized India as a mighty and dynamic power, with three hundred million faces, irradiated with light and vigor from a single mighty heart. The thought and meaning of India's message seemed one to Bharati, though often expressed and sounded in eighteen different tongues. To the poet, his country's destiny is one and the same, because it is common to the entire population of the subcontinent. He wanted to formulate a great law then and there. If one among these millions of mouths should go unfed, the millions should lay waste the whole world. But when each one lives and works for all, all shall together make the entire world a heaven on earth.

Such is Bharati's blue print for national integration. The warmth of sentiment and flow of thought as expressed here are all to be found in the beatific vision of the poet as crystallized from time to time in the outpouring of his soul through the medium of his songs and writings.

While yet India was in bondage he saw the glories that were to be hers in the days to come. He wrote:

> With six hundred million doughty arms
> Mother India shall enforce righteous rule;
> When foes dare her right to cross
> She will pulverise them into dust.

India henceforth will have only one prayer on her lips while serving humanity with all her might. And that prayer shall be addressed to Heaven:

> Make my arms mighty for service
> My thoughts mighty for love
> Such means will immortality ensure
> In the coming era of human evolution.

In another poem, "New Birth," a fitting epitome for what his patriotism stood for, he says:

> Ring all temple bells for India is born again.
> Her new name is the one that she had long, long ago
> Bharat.
> Great is her thirst for new things
>
> Ring all temple bells
> The re-born Mother has begun to speak, to sing and dance.
> She plays, the infant Devi,
> daughter of old Himalayas, the pre-destined
> bride of Shiva, the great God. . . .
>
> Oh, ring all temple bells.
> Make feast and festivals.
>
> The Mother is gaining secular knowledge.
> She is learning arts, sciences, trades.
> Behold her excelling astonished teachers
> Behold how she teaches under pretence of being taught.
> Oh ring, ring, ring, ring, all the temple bells.

Bharati's fiery patriotic writings have not lost their magic spell. They still provide inspiration, courage, confidence, faith, consolation, and serenity when needed, because his ideas are of great national significance since they help to infuse national consciousness and pride in the people of India.

CHAPTER 6

Religious Poetry

"THEY dreamt not of a perishable home / Who thus could build."
So sang Wordsworth amid the glories of King's College Chapel,
Cambridge. He meant that the builders of that noble fane were men
of spiritual vision and living faith, men whose eyes were fixed upon
the eternal archetype, the "pattern laid up in the heavens," for which
they struggled to find a material embodiment. This heavenly pattern
is not that of commercial prosperity or military prowess, but rather
the measure in which it bodies forth the eternal truth and goodness
and beauty that lie at the unseen heart of the world; and its greatest
builders, in like manner, are those who themselves have seen the
heavenly vision and can open the eyes of others to see it too.

If this be true, then assuredly we are right in giving Subramanya
Bharati his rightful place among such men of faith for whom the unseen verities are far more evident and more sure than the passing
shows of the world. Both by the witness of his life and character and
through the magic of his poetry he was able to share with others the
vision which was his own unfailing inspiration. Bharati was blessed
with a creative coinage of idiom and expression. His religious poetry
has a clear individuality of its own, growing like an iridescent spirit
of outspoken frankness. Truth shines supreme and clear throughout
his religious verse which is embedded in a superb prosody of thought-
ful profoundity. When stirred to proclamation, Bharati excels many
a poet in the arrangement of words under the symmetry of emotional
splendor.

Bharati was a poet imbued with an unquenching thirst for God. He
was essentially a monotheist, though pantheistic in approach. In one
of his poems he gives a very eclectic definition of God, acceptable to
men of all denominations. The poem is noted for both the loftiness of
ideas and the words employed. A close English rendering would run
thus:

What is that which of grace is full
Which is neither here nor there only,
But everywhere as the fullness of peace!

What is that which willing myriads
Of worlds to float in the expanse of the space,
Is the life of all things?

What is that which the mind
Cannot grasp and speech cannot define?

What is that which exists impartially,
While countless creeds in every land claim it
Each its own?

Amid such contending claims,
What is that which endlessly is knowledge, love, and power?

What is that whose bourne is without day or night
That indeed is soul satisfying?

That let us worship, deeming all things visible as
Phenomena in the expanse of the silent spirit.

It was Bharati who said "Not an atom moves but by His will."
The epithets used by the poet to describe God are innumerable. In essence, he conceived God as an absolute existence *(Sat)*, consciousness
(Chit), and bliss *(Ananda)* and as the source of all power and light. In
the words of Prof. T. P. Meenakshisundaram Pillai "eclecticism
shines through his poems in spite of his passing reference to sectarian
outlook."[1]

The theme of supplicating God for His grace runs throughout
Bharati's poetry. He believes that God is One and that man should be
conscious of this fact. His religion of universal love as exemplified by
his depiction of love is very well portrayed in another of his widely
read poems:

Mountain-like as Thou art,
Thou art in the hand grip called love.
Treasure-like as Thou art,
Thou art caught in the net called love.
Ambrosia-like as Thou art,
Thou art in the hollow of the palm called love.

He stresses the oneness of various religions and how the world should live with a feeling of one religion or under one creed. He says,

> The bright presence sitting
> In contemplation, wearing
> The crescent moon and Athi blossom
> The dark one that sleeps on the sea
> The one that enlightened Prophet Mohammed
> And the one worshipped
> As the father of Jesus
> All these idealized by
> Many religions prove to be
> One same pervading reality.

By this he preaches that all religions are one, and men should live in harmony, uniting all into one universal religion. "Bharati is also fond of quoting from the Bible, Quran and various Sikh, Buddhist and Jain scriptures."[2] Saturated with Indian culture, he often quotes from the golden precepts of Indian saints even as he lends charm and breathes life into his contributions. It is his pious wish that all men should live together forgetting their distinctions of caste, creed, and religion and considering even the inferior creatures like birds and animals as their friends. He points out that not only the lowborn, but even animals like pigs and asses should be loved, for God dwells in them as well as in other things.

> Hear my disciple! On seeing
> An ass, a pig, or a scorpion
> We must raise our hands overhead
> And prostrate calling Sankara! Sankara!

He does not stop with making humanity live happily. He estimates all creations as one race, which should live together with joy and plenty. Calling every creation of God as man's kith and kin, he sings:

> Crows and birds are our race
> The vast sea and hills, our tribe
> Where ever we turn, we see only ourselves
> The more we see around, the greater is ecstasy.

Time and again he stresses that man's life — life in the world and in the soul — blossoms only by love, and cruelty and wickedness prop up their heads only because of the want of love in the human heart. "All men in this world are like brothers to each other," he stated, emphasizing the world fraternity — universal brotherhood. He sings about this brotherhood in these lines:

> Equality in the world
> Will lead to fraternity
> Will not harm anyone
> But will liberate all the world.

Yes, if all live, bound by a brotherly affection and without any difference or distinction, where will be any harm or evil? Where will be cruelty? Where will be war? Where can we find misery and pain? Bharati calls a sinner anyone who teaches the distinction of high and low birth. He calls the evils of casteism a disease which man has invented and with which man has learned how to live a life tainted by parochialism and narrow-mindedness. Bharati attacks various castes based on profession or work, by which men have created a wall of segregation among themselves. He proclaims "Hence evils of caste — / The world / Shall prosper on love." In another poem he says: "The time is past when we paid respect to big birth / Now the so-called low men are equal with us."

According to Prof T. P. Meenakshisundaram Pillai, "His religion of universal love unfortunately came before people were ripe for it. He did not have a Vivekananda to deliver the message in English."[3] Nevertheless Bharati was fortunate in having been around at a time when people were just awakening to these social evils.

Bharati plunges into the future as often he flees back to the Vedic seers to be one with them in worshipping the Sun and the Wind, the Moon and the Stars, the Rain and the Fire — all converging no doubt upon the one theme of a Supreme awareness of a higher power which is manifest in all elements and yet not of them, but transcending them. His Vedic culture had deeply inculcated in him a sense of the immensity of which he was an indivisible part. A passage on "Joy" is worth recollecting in this context:

> Now to the passage about joy or sweetness:
> The world is sweet. The sky is full of it.
> The wind also is of the same kind.
> Fire is sweet. Water is sweet. Earth is sweet.
> The Sun is good. So also the moon.
> The stars of the heavens are all very sweet.

> Rain is sweet. Lightning is sweet. Thunder is sweet.
> Sea is sweet. Mountain is sweet. Forests are sweet.

One to whom lightning and thunder can be enjoyable cannot be of the mere commonplace variety. He must be one who has transcended normal capacities and derived from everything around him a sense of joy and fulfillment. In short, Bharati was a man of self-realization and of oneness with all creation. He was definitely lost in contemplation and moods of penance, for otherwise the splendid visions he had of Parasakti (goddess of power) could not have been vouchsafed to him in his most intense dreams: "The state of sorrowlessness is Sakti / The perennial awakening is Sakti / Tenderness seasoned with Love is Sakti / Fulfillment of manliness is Sakti."

He burst forth also into many lines of self-dedication to Kali. The pictures he had painted and the image he had gathered of the Mother indicate the experiences of exaltation of spirit and of his own identification with a higher power. Without conceding him some sort of self-realization, the following lines would defeat understanding: "I saw her in the moonlight bright. / Refuge in Thee I cried forthright, / I have quelled my senses all / I have killed the Self with all." Again, an exhortation to his great deity runs as follows: "Illumine this thought of mine; / If not reduce this body to death's decay." His fulfillment he has recorded in these words:

> This mind and this understanding of mine,
> Waited twenty-seven long years.
> Thanks to Thee, O Mother great!
> My hallucinations have vanished.
> Hence my service hereafter will be only to Thee.

"After his Pondicherry exile Bharati was *en rapport* with a higher consciousness,"[4] and in a mood of utter poise of the mind he broke into enlivening songs of unapproachable felicity.

> Parasakti's ordinance is supreme.
> She saves us from the sea rolling her waves
> Over us.
> May her name ever endure.

According to Bharati's religion, this world is all alike, the play of the Mother and everybody is an instrument, a toy or a lute in Her hands. He instinctively recognized the Mother as present in evil, terror, sorrow, and annihilation as well as in that which makes for sweetness and joy. Bharati worships the Mother in all aspects and expresses his inarticulate feelings and aspirations of his soul through his religious songs that have an abiding and deep hold on us. His choice of words, the turn of phrases and the structure of stanzas, the peculiar and appropriate rhythm and cadence are all aglow with the exquisite brilliance of his creative art.

Next in importance come his matchless songs in praise of Krishna. He lavishes all his gifts of song on the boyhood pranks and youthful sports of the divine cowherd with the village belles. In these songs, the lover-beloved conception rises into striking prominence. Lord Krishna is frequently referred to as the lover, the individual soul as the beloved, and sometimes vice versa. This type of Bharati's poetry seems to be love poetry of a sensuous kind, but in reality it has only a paramount symbolical and spiritual meaning and no other. He has written exquisite songs in this pattern and has to his credit a conception of Krishna in all human relationships such as Father, Mother, Child, Teacher and Servant.

Among the Gods worshipped by Tamil Hindus, Muruga or Subramanya is especially beloved by them; he has a number of ancient hill temples dedicated to Him. The puranic account of the origin of this God, his exploit in destroying the demon Surapadman, his self-confidence which made him a mentor to his father Lord Siva, and his two marriages to Valli and Deivayanai have thrown a halo of sacred romance around this God and evoked some of the finest and most perfect lyrics from Bharati expressing his devotion and love.

Bharati's poems on Goddesses Lakshmi and Saraswati are of a high order. They contain many profound ideas on art and religion. In a song on Lakshmi, the poet says:

> Come, let us sing her praises,
> bless her feet and climb the heights of power.
> Behold her in gold and gems, in flower and incense;
> In the lamp and virgin's smile;
> In luxurious woodlands, groves and fields;
> In the will that dares,
> And in royal lineaments.
>
> Dedicate unto her grace all knowledge that you have;
> Attain to her splendors, and vanquish dire want;
> Rise high in the world by joyous affirmation of Lakshmi,

who is revealed,
In conquering armies and the traffic of the far-sighted,
In self control, and say, in the harmonious lays of her
poet-votaries,
Come, let us affirm the energy of Vishnu, the jewel of
the crimson flower, Lakshmi.

There are a considerable number of poems of great power and
appeal — such as "Why Do You Cover Your Eyes?" — in which
Bharati has given expression to his religious philosophy. He claims
that the idea of God as knowledge is straightforward and to the
point, and he complains that the devotee's form of worship covers his
eyes to this fact. Perhaps the point is that the devotee loves long
stories, elaborate temples and images, rituals and hymns, songs,
dances, and poses and yet seems to lack any real philosophical approach, because in spite of the devotee's adoration, he is unable to
see God in his real manifestation.

Devotion first asks, "Are you straight and to the point?
When I was Sita, you took fourteen years and much rambling
to reach me.
When I was Arjun, you took eighteen chapters to tell me what
you could have in one metre.
When I was Prahlad, you came promptly no doubt out of a pillar
but lost your temper for a long time and I was hard put to it
to calm down.
When I was Yasodhara, it took you many years to come my way
and even then you took long to understand me and give me your
blessings.
I never close my eyes.
As Sita, my eyes were with my heart and that was with You. It
was Ravan who closed his eyes to greatness, in spite of all his
scholarship.
As Arjun, I was never tired of seeing your eyes and in fact
received *divya drishti* from you. It was Dritharashtra who
was blind in spite of his being the Emperor of India.
As Prahlad, I saw what was coming. I saw what was happening.
I saw you as you were. It was my father who did not see until
it was too late.
As Yasodhara, I saw you and nothing else. In fact, there was
nothing else for me to see. It was some of your disciples who
failed to see your soul of compassion.
And then did I shut my eyes of you? When I was Sita,

you closed your eyes to justice and fair play and love
and sent me out of sight.

. . . .

When I was Prahlad, when you ultimately calmed down,
You closed your eyes and slept like a true lion and
bad lover. May be you are still asleep.
When I was Yasodhara you sat still with eyes closed
or wrapt in deep meditation, so that your disciples
preached and did what they liked in your name.
To a person who closed his eyes, everyone in the world
appears to have closed his eyes. Oh God of all Gods,
eyes or no eyes, I love you.

Within the earth as Sita,
Ruling the earth as Arjun,
Serving the earth as Prahlad,
Loving the earth as Yasodhara,
I have you,
I have you,
I love you,
I love you,

Thus in a world spiritually short-sighted, almost to the point of
blindness, Bharati has given the best of vision, and better still, the
spirit of devotion. His choice of four names is a stroke of genius. Sita
as the ideal devotee represents the cream of the *Ramayana*. Arjun as
the typical man, represents the arrow mark of *Mahabharata* and
receives the message of the *Gita* from Krishna who is Narayana, the
goal of man. Prahlad as the ideal devotee, represents the big question
mark of revolution in the Puranas. Yasodhara as the ideal consort of
the Buddha represents "The Light of Asia."

From another point of view, Bharati has given equal representa-
tion to the male and female spirits in devotion. He has given the best
and noblest interpretation of the greater Indian life, culture, and
religion and has given a novel group photograph of the spirit of India, as should be seen by the present and future generations. It is
tempting to imagine oneself as Sri Rama, Sri Krishna, Nrisimha,
and Buddha. It is heroic to take the part of Sita, Arjun, Prahlad, and
Yasodhara.

Bharati was a believer in the pristine and dynamic Hinduism of the
early Vedic and Upanishadic seers. Though he owed allegiance to the
Bhagavad Gita and the doctrine of *Karma*, he rejected the latter day

Puranic Hinduism with its innumerable rituals, caste taboos, and social regulations. However, he fully realized "the poetic and cultural value of the great and massive Puranic literature of Hinduism, proof of which is to be had in every page of his writings more especially in his 'Sixty six.' "[5] It is a remarkable poem consisting of sixty-six stanzas; and each stanza tells of his dauntless adventures in the realm of the spirit with a rare charm and beauty of its own.

Bharati sings that he belongs to a mighty race of Siddhas — a sect that is bent on triumphing over death. The language which he wields smacks of the peculiar jargon which has often been employed in Tamil religious literature. The Universal Mother has transfigured herself into a rare flower in the fair garden of love and has made him a bee so that he can drink to the lees its honey and enjoy its sweet divine fragrance. The whole creation is her endless sport. It is She that pours through Bharati the rich wine of song.

The wise who have sung of the glories of immortality have all perished. Neither the Buddha, nor Sankara nor Ramanuja is able to withstand the tide of time that has swept them all into the vast gulf of death. Jesus Christ is nailed on the bitter cross and dies. Rama falls into the sweeping waters of the Sarayu, and Krishna dies of the fatal wound of an arrow. Bharati dreams of a deathless state and endeavors to find a way out of the jaws of death. In *Back to the Methusalah* Bernard Shaw says that one may prolong one's life by the sheer will to live. A complete triumph over death is the dream of a Ramalinga Swamigal and an Aurobindo. Neither Ramalinga Swamigal nor Aurobindo nor Bharati himself has succeeded; but the ideal is there shining in the distant horizon attracting the daring and master spirits of every age. Bharati believes that if anger and lust were to be slain, the doors of immortality would be flung open to us, and the deadliest foe that blocks the path of realization is our all-consuming anger. What if millions have fallen prey to death; let us strive with all our might and main to search for the secret that can make us eternally young.

The great virtue of patience lies beyond the pale of one's understanding; its might beggars description. Bharati gives a new significance and savor to the everlasting hills of divine patience. Firmly seated on them we may laugh to scorn all the tempests of life and all the raging seas of miseries below. Bharati gives us a list of seers whom he has met in his life and who have infused into him the message of the *Vedas*. According to it God is the pen that writes and the word which it shapes. He makes us alive to the sacredness of woman in whom one must find the divine dance of the mother of us all.

In the *Vedas*, there is an eloquent plea for religious toleration; and all the myriad faiths which we behold on earth are but various paths that lead to the far-off shrine of the Lord. "Thou art that," "I am He" — this is the eternal message that Bharati delivers to the world. It is only the voice of the *Vedas* that rings through the long corridors of time. He also sings of bringing Heaven down on earth by human effort.

To him God was an intense reality pervading the entire universe. Though he was a true Hindu, his living faith in the higher doctrine of universal love made him love and respect all other peoples and religions. He sings of Allah, Buddha, Christ, and the Sikh Gurus with genuine reverence. The teaching "Love thine enemy" is the theme of a noble song of his:

> Love thine enemy, heart of mine, Oh!
> Love thine enemy.
>
> Hast thou not seen the shining flame
> Amidst the darkening smoke?
> In foeman's soul lives Krishna, whom
> As Love the wise invoke.
>
> Oft we have preached to men that God
> In all that is doth shine.
> Why, then, my heart, 'tis God that stands
> Arrayed as foemen's line.
>
> Dost know that limpid pearls are found
> Within the oyster vile?
> Hast seen on dunghill, too, sometimes
> The starry blossom smile?
>
> The heart that fans its wrath, shall it
> The inner peace possess?
> The honey-poison mixed, shall it
> Be wholesome nevertheless?
>
> Shall we who strive for Life and Growth,
> Lend thought to Sad Decay?
> "Thine evil thoughts recoil on thee,"
> So do the wise ones say.

When Arjun fought, 'twas Krishna whom
He faced, disguised as foes;
'Twas Krishna, too, that drove his car
In charioteering pose.

Strike not the tiger threatening thee,
But love it straight and true;
The Mother of All hath donned that garb
Salute her there, there too.

Love thine enemy, heart of mine, Oh!
Love thine enemy.

C. Viswanath Iyer, the poet's younger brother, asserts in a well-written monograph that Bharati was "more in the tradition of the Rishis, the Drashta [Seer of the Mantra] than in that of the Smritikar [writer from memory] or a Bhashyakar [Commentator] or a saint." A close and careful study of his religious poems lends color to this view, if we also take into account the way in which Bharati braved many difficulties in his life of storm, stress, and political turmoil and led a life of robust optimism and joy composing songs and poems.

CHAPTER 7

Mysticism

ALTHOUGH Subramanya Bharati is a staunch advocate of supramental knowledge, he cannot be classed as a philosopher in the general sense of the term. He is a mystic in the real sense. He is a true seeker of knowledge. His is the most practical and living mysticism and if because of this practical and living nature of his mysticism he is called a philosopher, we have nothing to grudge him. Bharati's mysticism is not the mysticism of ordinary savants who try to rise individually to the supramental plane, but who — even when they succeed — fail to bring anything down that can be made a permanent part of human consciousness. Bharati's mysticism is the mysticism of the Yoga, where the physical and the supraphysical meet. It is a double movement of ascent and descent. This mysticism promises a thorough transformation of normal consciousness into supermind. It is never opposed to reason or intellect; it is not fleeting and evanescent, for in the supramental plane the higher knowledge is permanent, and it is never confined to subjective certainty but admits of objective validity, because "the less perfect intuition must be perfected by one more perfect." "Bharati's mysticism then should not be called philosophy, as we ordinarily understand it. It is a living mysticism, a practical one, truly representing the Indian heritage."[1]

Bharati added his own freshness to devotional mysticism when he dispensed with all mythological symbols and sectarian concepts of God. He preferred his own spiritual longings to the knowledge gathered from legends and Puranic stories. No mean fervor does he arouse in us when he makes his Kannan (Krishna) live before our eyes in all the varying charms of childhood or youth. He makes his Kannan the woman, or even the servant, and the human soul plays the part of both a man and a master. In Tamil literature it is not difficult to see that this conception of love as a way of life lends itself to a wide range of symbolic application, with the beloved as the symbol of a man's ideals in life and his constancy to her as the symbol of his constancy to those ideals. As might be expected in Indian society, it was to the sphere of religion that this transference of the experiences and the value of earthly love was first made. Long before Suka Brahman, in his ecstatic moods of God-Realization, chose to surpass all known theistic philosophy by resorting to the soulful strains of Radha and Krishna, Tamil poetry was moving simultaneously on two levels, so that almost any line might be interpreted as an expression either of a man's love for his mistress or, in the mystic sense, of the worshipper's love for his God. Love was divided into two categories — symbolic love and real love — and it is again characteristic of the Indian mind that contrary to what people in the West would expect, it was earthly love which was characterized as symbolic, and mystic love which was called real.

The idea that man's passionate love for a woman and his love for his God are two closely parallel experiences has long been unfamiliar to the Western world, and it is not easily reacquired. In the West, people are inhibited by a strong Protestant tradition, which tends to regard sexual love as sinful, or if not sinful, at least not religious, and for this and other reasons they feel very uncomfortable with the symbolic identification of God with an irresistibly beautiful woman. They would do well to remember that it did not occur to their ancestors — not even to some of their Protestant ancestors — that there is anything objectionable in the parallelism between sexual and divine love. Thus in the Bible, in the Song of Solomon, we find that the chapter headings take the most sensuous descriptions of the beloved — her feet, her thighs, her belly, her navel, her breasts — as Christ's description of the graces of the Church. This treatment is not exceptional. J. M. Cohen in his *History of Western Literature* speaks of love poetry "translated a *lo divino* for pious reading, according to the strange custom of the time, with a divine lover carefully substituted on all occasions for an earthly one."[2] True, Bharati's symbolism at times is also reversed and God is not the beloved but the lover. However, this symbolism is also commonly found. The most notable instance is in Dante's *Divine Comedy,* where the figure of Beatrice appears both as Dante's earthly beloved and on other occasions as the symbol of Christ. Even the *Romance of the Rose* — that celebrated love poem — "was read by some in the divine sense, with the rose as a symbol of Jesus."[3]

Once this symbolic identification of God with the mistress is accepted, the recurring parallels between earthly and divine love are not difficult to grasp. For the starting point of all mysticism is that true religion is inconceivable without a direct and intimate relationship between man and his God, and that this relationship comes into being, like earthly love, through a process which is experienced with overwhelming intensity, and which in the last resort cannot be reasoned about. In both loves there is the same yearning for union with the beloved, the same striving for perfect constancy, the same unhesitating submission to the beloved's will — even where that will seems to be cruel and capricious — the same readiness to sacrifice even life itself where love demands that price.

It is not difficult to see that mysticism is potentially a subversive doctrine, and therefore deeply suspect. For if a man's one overriding aim in life is to draw even closer to his God, then the people of this world are unimportant in his eyes. If he relies upon his love of God to guide him, he does not need the guidance of learned divines and cannot accept their pretensions to be in some special sense the guardians of true religion; and this attitude of the mystic is not shared by a majority. Hindu mysticism has a wide range of expression, and it should not be thought that this potentially subversive trend in it was everywhere made explicit, still less that it was the dominant trend in Hindu mysticism as a whole. But in the convention of Tamil Vaishnavite or Saivite songs it does dominate, and it is not only made explicit but, like almost everything else in such songs, is carried to an extreme; and piecing together the lines of Bharati's songs, we can trace the logic of its development.

To Bharati the essence of religion is man's love of God, a love as all-consuming as love for a beautiful mistress. Rituals of worship are to him of no significance, and at this point his clash with orthodoxy begins. To Bharati, such rituals are good only if they are an aid to the expression of his love for God; they are meaningless if they are performed as a mere ritual, and positively harmful if they give rise in the poet's heart to the Pharisee's satisfaction that he is "not as other men are." So Bharati says:

> If pilgrimage could make a man a man
> Then all the world might make the pilgrimage.
> But that caste-ridden Brahmin is just back, and look at him —
> An ass he went; an ass he has returned.

As a mystic, Bharati declares that God is known in many forms and worshipped under different names by different creeds whose hearts are filled with passionate love for Him, and who dedicate themselves wholly to doing His will, no matter in what form or under what name they conceive of Him. In this community, differences of formal creed are of no account. "It is the power of His beauty that fills the world with light, / Be it the Church's candle or the lamp that lights Somnath." The idea of God's radiant beauty occurs again and again in Bharati. God manifests himself in the universe as in a great mirror. He is immanent in all things, and the true love may adore Him in His handiwork:

> Tell me, what else exists but He?
> To him who has the eyes to see
> The day, the sun, the night, the moon
> Show forth His forms, His Majesty.
> Manifest, hidden, first and last
> Is He, is He, is He, is He.

And it follows that reverence for God's creation is as incumbent on the true Hindu as is reverence for the *Bhagavad Gita*, every verse of which is His authentic word, for "The atoms that compose the universe / Are verses written by the hand of God."

The example of the universe itself shows man the way, for it is inspired with unceasing love and adoration of the Divine Beloved, its Creator. The stars shine like the bright eyes of the lover gazing expectantly in the direction from which he expects his beloved to come: "Whose coming do they look for, O Lord? The stars, bright shining / Gaze on in all their thousands, wide eyed, night after night." The waves of the sea rise and fall like a lover repeatedly trying and repeatedly failing, to draw his mistress into his embrace: "Its every wave is rising up as though to clasp its love; / Who is it whom the ocean thus seeks ever to embrace?" To love and to worship the beauty of the universe is to worship God, whose manifestation that beauty is: "The world of beauty is a wondrous world; / A man must fall in love with that world too." But God's very self-sufficiency is a ground for suspicion and complaint: "To God I have committed all my purposes — and yet / My heart misgives me; is He not a law unto Himself?"

The same awareness of man's unique potentialities and of the unique honor he should enjoy in God's universe dictates the relations that should prevail between man and man. Bharati believes that the essence of true religion can be summed up in the commandment not to injure your fellowmen, and that formal religion is unimportant by comparison:

> Go to the temple; ring all its bells —
> Live all your days with drunkards in their den —
> Do anything you want to do my friend,
> But do not seek to harm your fellow men.

Another verse stresses the same point: "When have I said to you, 'Do this!' or 'Don't do that!' / No, only try to make more room within your heart, there is no other law." Many more verses elaborate these general commandments. To obey them we must eradicate from our hearts all arrogance towards Him, and bring in humility in its place:

> Here in this world of dust look to your honor.
> Head high in pride, you care not where you tread.
> See how the flood, which makes the desert blossom
> Moves over on its path with lowered head.

The ideal is to develop our sensitivity so that we feel another's pain as though it were our own. Often Bharati compares man in his distress to a songbird imprisoned in a cage, and says: "I heard the lamentation of the prisoner in his cage . . . / It was my heart that ached, and I that was held captive there." If it were in Bharati's power, he would make all men happy: "All the country would thrive and teem with life — / Alas! if only I controlled the means!"

If we can once fill our hearts with the love of our fellowmen, we will inspire an equal love in the other's heart, and we will then see a miracle performed. For when love possesses it, that same heart which was once as brittle as glass becomes so strong that no power can assail it. No longer it is a palace defenseless against those who would destroy it: "Palace and gate and roof and brick and clay — none of them last; / So make the humble heart the strong foundation of your house." Or else "Live in the heart; make it your home; for the Great Architect / Has never built a dwelling so acceptable as this."

Verses like these depict the heart possessed by love as a power that stands immovable against every conceivable force. But it is something more than that; it is itself a force or irresistible power: "This heart which seems no greater than a single drop of blood / Is like a whirlwind mingling earth and heaven with its force." For the heart bears all, but conquers all. Physically small though it is, its capacities are as great as the ocean, as vast as the great expanses of land. And this is why the heart — the seat of love, the throne of the Divine Beloved, the heart infinitely sensitive and yet infinitely strong — is our surest guide in life: "Love was our faith, this heart our guide along the path we trod; / This heart was our preceptor, this our Guru, this our God." It is "our Guru" and "our God" because the bidding of the heart *is* the bidding of the Guru and of God.

Yet the man who would follow its dictates implicitly clashes inevitably with the pillars of society and with the men of the world. To men in authority the good man is he who submits to their legal or rightful power and obeys their will. But no authority looks kindly upon those who rule their life not by outside commands but by the voice of God, which speaks to their hearts and tells them that love — love of God and love of neighbors — must be the sole guiding force. Neither the wealth of the nation nor the learning of divines impresses such men; both are quite irrelevant to their task in life: "What do you need to render what is due? / Nor wealth nor learning enters [into] it."

The clash with the man of the world is equally unavoidable. For the man of the world prides himself on his practical wisdom, on accepting the world as it is, on taking the view that high principles are all very well, but that a man has to make his way in the world, and in the practical business of life it is madness to bring principles into it. To this argument Bharati replies, in effect, that if the way of life is sanity, then give him madness every time. For this madness is, once again, the madness of the lover, the way of life of the man so possessed by love for his God or his ideals that he remains true to it no matter what men who lack the capacity to comprehend it may think of him or do to him. Such madness is a source of both joy and pride to Bharati, for it teaches a wisdom incomparably higher than that produced in the hard heads of practical men, and any lapse into their sanity and good sense is something to regret: "Good sense has come to fetter me. Before that / I knew the joy of life, for I was mad." Bharati knows as well as the man of the world that this is the way not to worldly success but to poverty and destitution. The world does not treat kindly those who do not conform to its ways; Fate does not befriend such men, and it is the height of simplicity to expect it to: "It made and marred a thousand such as you. / Don't be so simple: Fate is not your friend."

Enough has already been said to show that Bharati's mysticism or his "religion of love," has its own commandments, and that these more often than not clash head on with the commandments of orthodox Hinduism. It would be an understatement to say that no attempt is made to avoid this clash. Bharati's mysticism is the extreme, radical mysticism which orthodox Hindus abhorred, hated, and persecuted; and his loathing was most cordially returned. In the ceaseless warfare that followed, each side pushed its position to extremes. Bharati had started from the point that the prescribed Hindu duties of prayer, fasting, almsgiving, and pilgrimage were at best of limited value in helping him to cultivate the all-important love for God, and could be harmful if their ritual performance became a substitute for true religion and a source of self-righteousness. He now took the unequivocal view that they were always harmful, the source of bigotry and self-satisfaction, and nothing else; and he took the position that not only must he not perform them but he must openly flout them.

But though Bharati revered the mystics he did not follow those among them who withdrew from the world to live in solitary contemplation of God. He writes: "You must live in the world, where griefs and joys beset you — / And live to such effect that men may not forget you." Out of his heart flowed song after song charged with the purest love of God which a mystic has; and love is self-surrender. In one such song, the poet sings:

> Surrender unto Him
> Thy body and thy soul,
> All thou art and all thou hast!
> Love Him, love not thyself!
> Think as He thinketh!
> Will as He willeth!
> Cling to His Lotus-feet alone!
> And the Beloved will accept thee!

Many of his songs are filled with this aspiration — to forget himself, to forget the world and to seek refuge at the Lotus feet of his one and only Krishna. It is the aspiration to surrender all we have and all we are to the One Life, to sit in silence and commune with the Beloved. And He is not afar: He is within us! Bharati expresses his longing thus:

> The world attracts me not!
> I yearn to sit at Thy Lotus feet,
> And be dyed in the dye of love.
> To live in Thee is life:

> To be afar from Thee is death!
> Keep me close,
> Very close to Thee,
> Beloved!

Sometimes the tone is more serious:

> My heart is stricken with illness:
> And my body a faded flower!
> Within me I carry the wounds
> Of love and longing for Thee,
> When wilt thou call me,
> O King of my heart?

The more serious tone of a verse such as this brings us back to the essential basis of mysticism, the essence of which is to love God with all our heart and soul. If we live by this religion, all other commandments are superseded; we may — indeed, we must — give full rein to every generous impulse within us, to everything which stimulates love and adoration; and if this sometimes leads us to excess, we can trust implicitly in God's infinite mercy to forgive us.

In Bharati's terminology "real love" — that is, divine love — embraces not only the love of God in the sense in which we understand it, but a complete dedication to our ideals in life, ideals which will serve to the end, no matter what suffering this may bring down upon us. Bharati did not distinguish between the service of God and the service of his ideals, for he saw his ideals as prescribed for him by God and his devotion to them as an integral part of his devotion to God. He allowed himself the unrestrained freedom to speak the truth about love and life as he saw it, and to attack the enemies of that truth in the sharpest terms. Society tolerated such frankness in poetry alone, and it was a freedom that Bharati treasured:

> I speak the secrets of my heart to old and young alike;
> My voice is free and unrestrained; and none can curb my tongue.

Bharati's mysticism is a compound of his belief in the holiness of beauty, his humanism, his refusal to compromise his principles for the sake of wordly advancement and his proud self-dedication to the highest ideals of life. Sometimes in the poems of exhortation he uses the first person for introducing his song "Where else can my soul find happiness (but in Kannan)?", and then goes on to make his general points — in this case, by asking a number of pointed rhetorical questions. To quote one such verse:

> Now I have danced too much, Kannan,
> Wearing the garment of lust and anger,
> On my neck a garland of sensuality.
> The ankle bells of delusion peal out sweet words of malice;
> Envy sounds in my body in all kinds of beats.
> Sunk in error, my mind has become a drum that keeps bad time.
> My waist is tied with the sash of illusion,
> I wear the mark of greed on my forehead.
> Fully warmed up, I have demonstrated hundreds of
> Dance techniques, oblivious to land, sea and time.
> O Nandalala, take away my ignorance.

Bharati is fond of that expressive repetition of words which is one of the characteristics of Tamil idiom, and which conveys either emphasis or distribution in time or space or both. Only occasionally can one hope to convey anything like the full effect in English. In a line which may be taken equally well either in the literal or in the mystic sense he says: "I seek you like the morning breeze that with each dawn goes forth again / From house to house, from door to door, from town to town, from lane to lane." Many other examples are quite untranslatable. A similar liking for this style of expression is evident in the many verses where the whole force is achieved by piling word upon word: "The Mother came but once, but do not ask what left me as She went: / My strength, and faith, and fortitude, and will, and heart and soul."

Bharati's mystic verse as a whole makes clear his conception that not only are all aspects of his spiritual experience relevant to one another; they are all aspects of what is to him essentially the same experience, the experience of a man driven by the single force of love, manifesting itself simultaneously in love of God, love of his fellowmen, and love of a high ideal in life, as well as in the indomitable power to resist unbroken the persecution of the enemies of love in all these fields. His voice is closer than that of any other Tamil poet to the voice of the mystic and, in language and feeling, closer to some of the European mystics. In this respect he perhaps outshines several past mystic poets of the subcontinent such as Mirabai, Kabir, Surdas, and his fellow Krishnaite poets. Bharati's mysticism takes expression in his poetry of a single integral outlook, which gives it its powerful appeal.

CHAPTER 8

Place in Tamil Literature

"WITH the prowess of my songs / The Universe shall I rule" Thus sang Bharati, the bard of resurgent Tamilnadu who has introduced, in accordance with the spirit of the times, a new theme of poetry. "The songs of patriotism or national songs are new to Tamil literature in the way they have been elaborated by him."[1] In early Tamil literature there may have been poems expressing loyalty to the king as representing the nation, culture, or religion, but in Bharati's national songs, the loyalty is to the nation and to the people. In the Freedom fight, thousands of people with Bharati's songs on their lips faced British bullets and worse during the fight for freedom. The poet's spirit refused to bow to the insolent might of the Raj and from his pen flashed forth songs of fiery patriotism which were trend setters in Tamil poetical literature. Bharati's poems particularly glorified the culture and language of the Tamils. There is that joy of the memory of the past in his prosody which had never before come out in Tamil poetry. He did not recollect all those as a mere dream of the past, but as the living inspiration of the present and the future. Neither language nor culture was a distant vision for him. He made Tamilians see India not in Delhi, Benares, or Madras but in the trees, in the fields, and in the rivers all round them. For him, the divine language was not merely enshrined in cadjen leaves but in the songs of the women, the plays of children, and the oft-repeated proverbs and phrases of the common people. Unlike the Sangam poets, Bharati saw divinity in every atom of the soil and in every man and woman. He saw God in ordinary life, in friends, in lovers, in teachers. No wonder, therefore, that this new theme and new trend in poetry received new rhythm and a new meter. This old theme became new only in the sense that the divinity and glory of the people are new when they are discovered anew. In this way too such old themes as Vedic mysticism became new in Bharati's verse, both in their inspiration and expression.

Bharati heralded a social revolution by this metrical revolution. He made Tamilians feel equality and fraternity, while proclaiming independence and liberty. This kinship to Mother India made all Tamilnadu belong to one great Indian family. His nationalism and newer contacts with a wider world of humanity transformed the poet in him to a patriot of the first rank and a poet of perennial importance. His attempt to raise both himself and his people is what distinguishes him from a previous age of saints and savants. An exclusive sense of self-fulfillment and a heaven of his own making was something he hated, as Tagore and Gandhi similarly felt and expressed at various times. To serve the humble and raise the downtrodden are as much sources of deliverance for a soul as renunciation and a religious life. Bharati believed in a religion that equally suffused Swami Vivekananda to exclaim "All of us are going towards the same goal. The difference between virtue and vice is one of degree; the difference between strength and weakness is one of degree; the difference between heaven and hell is one of degree; the difference between life and death is one of degree; all differences in this world are of degrees and not of kind; because *oneness is the secret of everything.*"[2]

The result of his thought and his intense love of mankind made Bharati aim at a language shorn of all ornamental excesses:

> My songs have put off their adornments.
> They have no more desire for dress and decoration
> They mar our union;
> They come between You and me;
> Their jingle drowns your whispers.

The poet realised at an early age that even sounds of rhymes and phrases can wean away the genuine heart from reality and the substance of truth. His verse marks a stage in Tamil poetry when even figures of speech and the usual employment of description strike as robbing the soul of its experience in expression. We may call it originality or by any other appellation, but Bharati's greatness is at the bottom of it.

"The part Bharati played by his life and writings as a valiant and tireless fighter for freedom in all its forms has, in a way, distracted attention from his contribution in revolutionizing Tamil poetry, in discovering for it new forms, rhythms, new poetic matter and a new poetic style."[3] This involved the colossal task of breaking through established literary conventions and tastes. In the fight for political and social freedom, Bharati was only one of a numerous band and not the most conspicuous figure in it, though, in the final analysis, his contribution to the success of the cause may be reckoned as great as that of any other hero. But in the Tamil literary field he was carrying on a one-man revolution. If after Bharati Tamil has not been what it was before him, the change was the result of his achievements in poetry, and this achievement was the outcome of deliberate planning and careful execution.

Phenomenal as Bharati's service to Tamil literature is in diverse ways, his greatest achievement was in freeing the language from pedantic acrobatics and bringing its literature to the bazaars and fields. His was an inspiring period in Indian history when the highly cultured but somnolent East came to a head-on clash with the aggressively pragmatic West, with its new idioms and values. Bharati was the symbol of this new awakening in Tamilnadu. In his poems he gave Tamilians their voice, their eyesight, their feelings, their consciousness, and their hopes and restored to them their very soul — all of which this ancient race of culture and civilization had lost and forgotten in its torpor of subjection. Bharati is the National poet of the Tamils in more senses than one. "His message plumbs the depths of all the varied seas of human life, and this is the universal aspect of Hinduism — his religion or rather of all true religions — the spirit which becomes the rhythm of all human activities, their moving force and direction."[4] This reveals the spiritual significance of his poetry which is again unique in the annals of Tamil literature; for he is a mystic in the best sense of the term.

Every poem of his reveals this bedrock from which he sings; but there are poems of his which proclaim themselves as Vedantic which are truly poetic incarnations of the spirit of universalism with its ever-expanding message to all kinds of human beings, ranging from children to mystics, all on march to Divine Perfection. We can mark four overlapping kinds or stages of poetry in Bharati which place him far ahead of all Tamil poets before him, including Kamban and Tiruvalluvar. There is first of all, reminding us of the lullaby of our infancy, the poetry which charms by its very music and rhythm, the words themselves — though sometimes present with varied repetitions and ringing patterns — playing no part except perhaps as appealing to the unconscious and the superconscious, as in all nursery rhymes. In the second stage, words and meanings become more and more important to the conscious mind itself, though with their echoes and reverberations traveling through the subconscious, where the hypnotic charm of music and rhythm still persists but only as the prop and echo of the sense. Here in this poetry, we get a picture or a dramatic speech — in any case a vision of the physical beauty or the mental joy — full of depth, color, and feeling coming withal with an unknown width which is the other name for universalism. This kind of poetry, as it were, is the quintessence of literature. It is poetry concentrating within its shortest dimensions a focal point of life. In the third stage comes a poetry embodying Bharati's message and his vision — his criticism of life as a whole in all its varied and variegated aspects — not as an abstract philosophy but as the living concrete incarnation of the message or vision in a story or drama. The story, whether new or old, may not be in perfect accord, for the message and vision may not grow or develop before our mental eye as it did with all the significance in the heart of hearts of Bharati. Therefore a fourth kind of poetry arises in which the story or drama embodying the message is the story of his own life seen as the universal story of life itself and of the spiritual progress of travel in the wonderland of mysticism. Dante's epic and the poems of Nammalwar and Manikkavacagar in Tamil literature are of this kind. But in Nammalwar and Manikkavacagar, the separate verses have an individuality and significance of their own, as in the second and sometimes in the first kind of Bharati's poetry. They form, as it were, a series of still pictures, sometimes ten verses to a picture, each series, by its very swift movement as in movies, creating before our mind's eye a moving drama of the spirit. Not so with Bharati who reminds us of stage directions more elaborate than in any drama and truly more poetic than elsewhere — something like the descriptions in Shakespeare who had in his day no scenic arrangements worthy of that name.

   It is true that Bharati has not attempted any comprehensive treatise in prose or verse on the nature of poetry in general, or on his own poetry. He was not in the habit of writing critical prefaces to editions of his poems setting forth the claims of a new poetry — which he was certainly or deliberately attempting — as many European poets like Dante, Wordsworth, and Arnold have done. Most of the time he was content with singing his lays and did not feel the need to defend them critically, or to point out the inner laws of their being. Yet, he undoubtedly meditated deeply on Tamil poetry and clearly worked out his own distinctive style and arrived at definite views as to what constitutes good poetry. The picture of Bharati that emerges out of all his writings is not that of an unconscious poet who by the intuitive power of genius stumbled upon good poetry that instantly appealed to the masses, but that of a singer "who had meditated long on the nature and purpose of his art and had formulated a complete theory of his own regarding his art."[5]

Bharati's conception of his own poetry comes out in brief indirect references and critical asides scattered throughout his works in verse and prose. From these references we can form a fairly good idea of what he thought of the nature of poetry in general and that of his own poetry in particular. He was painfully aware of the deplorable level to which Tamil poetry had sunk during the three or four centuries before him. He realized that it was the poets who were mainly to blame for this. They had not served their language or their public well. In his article on "Rebirth of India" he discusses this subject and analyzes the causes of the decay of poetry in Tamil:

> In our poetry the element of pleasure gradually began to disappear, and with it poetic delight. Our poets began to prefer the rough and thorny path to one level and smooth. As a result rubbish increased and poetry became uninteresting. Sincerity disappeared giving place to mere verbal embellishments. But the great Kamban thought differently when he compared the bright, clear, cool flow of the Godavari to great poetry.

Bharati explains with full approval Kamban's view that the language of poetry should have a sparkling brilliance; it should be clear; and it should have the cool, smooth flow of deep waters. He goes on to comment on the use of obsolete words in poetry and states that poetry should be written in language that can be clearly understood by the people of the time. Such is Bharati's poetry, a great new poetry — new in the poetic delight it provides, new in poetic matter, new in its poetic energy, and new in its style. He was quite conscious of the fact that he was "blazing new trails for Tamil poetry," as can be seen from one of his letters in verse to the Raja of Ettayapuram soliciting royal patronage.[6]

Bharati's work in changing the direction of Tamil poetry and in setting up new ideals for it reminds us of the efforts of Wordsworth and Coleridge who, between them, brought about a major revolution in English poetry, which is usually known as the Romantic Revolution. In the preface to the *Lyrical Ballads,* the manifesto of the new poetic revolution, Wordsworth lays claim to much the same things as Bharati does. Bharati's main achievement, as that of Wordsworth, was the discovery of new poetic matter and the creation of a new poetic style approximating the spoken language of the common man, free from artificial poetic diction.

Bharati had a clear analytical grasp of the elements that blend together to give great poetry. In his invocation to Vani, the Muse of Poetry, which opens the second canto of his *Panchali Sapatham*, he details the various functions of the poet in the right performance of which the Goddess must bless him. In his prayer he virtually describes what he considers to be the indispensable requirements of great poetry. They are a

clear grasp of the subject matter; lucidity of expression; the power of providing for those who subject the poem to deep study and thought, the higher imaginative pleasures through its profundity and suggestiveness; and powerful emotion that can move the reader even to the point of tears.

We have no means of ascertaining how far Bharati was acquainted with works in other languages. It is very likely that his indebtedness to others in this matter is very slight and he had developed his own style in the light of his own attitudes and experiences. It must be noted that Bharati was definitely of the view that a good poem does not carry all the wealth of its meaning on the surface so that a casual reader can carry off everything that it has to offer. A good poem offers its hidden pearls only to those who are prepared to dive deep for them. Through the use of imagery, through symbols, and through the connotative power of words, the poet can infinitely extend the scope of the meaning of his poem and reward closer study. Bharati is fully supported in this view by T. S. Eliot. To those who think that Bharati's poetry is great because it is extremely simple, so simple that even an uneducated reader can understand all that he has put into a poem, this view of poetry entertained by Bharati must sound strange. But is is always wiser and safer to believe what a poet says of poetry in general and of his own poetry in particular, and then to examine his poems to see if he follows his own rules. The popular belief that Bharati's poems are too simple and clear to call for minute study has resulted in a strange lack of good critical and scholarly studies of his works.

"There is practically no explanation in Tamil poetry before Bharati of the way in which the mechanism of a poet's mind works, the poetic process out of which a poem emerges."[7] Only poets can tell us about what happens inside them, and even among poets very few have been clearly aware of what is happening inside them when a poem is being born. Bharati is one of those few Tamil poets who were aware, and his account is very illuminating. He describes the poetic process in two poems on poetry. In the first of these he addresses poetry as his wedded wife and in the other as his sweetheart whom he is courting. He recalls the aching joys and dizzy raptures of the days of his courtship and laments the loss of poetic power when he had to give up his dedication to his love for the sake of seeking a living. The two figures of his wife and sweetheart provide him with excellent symbols to embody his views on poetry and his experiences as a poet.

The similes and metaphors which Bharati uses in speaking of poetry throw light on his poetic ideas. Poetry for Bharati is the golden pot filled with the immortal medicine of the gods. He is positively against the verbal embroidery that for long passed for poetry in Tamil. He discounts mere fine writing or wild flights of the imagination and highly decorative language. The classical virtues of enduring strength in construction and clarity in expressions are for him the prime requisites of a good poem. It was the invasion of these into the realm of poetry that had sapped the life of Tamil poetry in the later ages. The prime need of the hour was to free poetry from these encumbrances and to revitalize it and to bring poetry back into the lives of the common people. It was Bharati's firm faith that "a poet who can give us works written in simple diction, familiar style, rhythms that can be caught easily and tunes that the common people like, will be able to breathe new life into our mother tongue."

There is no doubt of his ambitions to perform this service for Tamil. He had a clear idea of what was needed for the task and he more than succeeded in accomplishing it, but it is not adequately recognized that his poetry is the result of a clearly thought-out program.

I *Prose Writings*

Bharati's eminence as a prose writer and his achievements in this field constitute a landmark in the development of modern Tamil prose. About thirty years ago, two fairly big volumes of Bharati's prose writings were brought out by Bharati Prachuralayam in Madras. One volume consists mainly of his journalistic writing of the period between 1907 and 1921 relating to political, social, and religious subjects. Even these, written in a hurry and in the heat of the moment have a fine literary flavor. The other volume contains his deliberate and mature prose.

To understand the real value and significance of Bharati's prose, it is necessary to consider briefly the development of prose in the Tamil language. In the works of the Sangam age, there is no prose at all, though there are some kinds of prose compositions in the most ancient Tamil grammar extant. While ancient Tamil men of letters wrote with profound knowledge, great insight, and incisive logic, they did not conceive of prose as a special literary art. Hence they did not develop fully the elements of syntax and form in their writing. Tamil prose before Bharati's time is one continuous stream of words, with sentences sometimes running to extreme length. Besides, the absence of punctuation, the scanty use of aids such as conjunctions, prepositions, etc., and a too full use of grammar have made it difficult even to read it freely, much less to understand it.

It was left to Subramanya Bharati, to "act boldly by removing such rigidity in prose and eliminating the use of archaic words, word-endings and phrase, found in Tamil prose in his writings."[8] He was the one who bridged the gap between written and spoken Tamil. Bharati correctly realized that the creation of modern Tamil literature mirroring the changing phases of the life of the people and their aspirations and the current intellectual and scientific knowledge would be impossible if the old way of Tamil writing was continued. He therefore marked out a new approach and successfully created a beautiful and powerful Tamil prose style, using the common speech so as to be within the comprehension of ordinary people. He did this without, however, a substantial break either with Tamil grammar or Tamil literary usages and traditions. This was a unique achievement unrivaled in the simplicity of style, lucidity of expression, and moving power of language, which often rises to poetical height and profundity of thought. His sweep of imagination in Tamil prose is indeed cosmic in its range and strength.

The chief qualities of Bharati's Tamil prose, besides its simplicity and lucidity, are verve, utter absence of stiffness or rigidity, easy flow, and rhythmic assonance. A careful reading of all his prose works shows that though he used Sanskrit words and did not strive to avoid them, there is an element of purity in his prose that adds strength and dignity to his style, because he has used words that are apt and easy to enunciate and understand, unlike present day purists who want to deliberately bring back into currency archaic words which have disappeared from use either in writing or speech in recent centuries. Bharati has expressed modern ideas with wonderful naturalness and ease. His prose writings are a model of what modern

Tamil literary prose should be, and they occupy an honored place in Tamil literature.

II *Development of Tamil Literature*

Subramanya Bharati was the first in Tamilnadu who liberated the Tamil language and its literature from all its chains and who paved a new way for further growth. In the words of Mu Varadarajan "Bharati is the father of the present era in Tamil. . . . He rescued Tamil literature from the stagnation of the matalayams and petty courts of zamindars and brought it into the main current of national life. The new epoch of renaissance in Tamil literature was ushered in with this great poet as its leader."[9]

Bharati contributed to the formation of modern Tamil literature in the first instance through his poetical creations but also through his critical remarks about language and literature with which he showed the way to other poets and writers. Though he never wrote on this problem continuously, he touched on it in different contexts in his prose articles and, now and then, in his poetry too. This can be explained by the fact that he drew up his ideas on different problems in the form of newspaper articles, with which he appealed to the broad masses. Inspired by the wish to awaken the national consciousness of the Tamilians he wrote also about language and literature as important factors for the national awakening of his country.

With deep regret Bharati points out again and again the stagnation of literature and other arts in Tamilnadu in comparison with the cultural rise in less backward parts of India. "We have started here to investigate the present condition of literature and other arts in Tamilnadu and the reasons for their being like that. The conclusions to which we come about Tamilnadu, are in general applicable to all other parts of India as well. While in Bengal and Maharashtra some of the fine arts are budding slowly, they are lifeless and stagnant in all the other parts of India. Let us now take Tamilnadu for instance. Are there now-a-days poets who can be compared to Kamban?"[10]

Continuing these considerations he turns to the various facts which blocked the growth of Tamil literature. In this connection he alludes to one phenomenon, which has been a hindrance for the evolution of literature not only in Tamilnadu, especially during the last centuries, but also in other Indian literatures.

"Those who are scholars and those who suppose themselves to be scholars, have started to write poems. Although scholarship to a certain extent is necessary for poets not all scholars possess the ability for writing poems; our people have forgotten this. Thus even the grammarians take it for a flaw in their fame, if they do not compose poems. So real poetry has disappeared in this land."[11]

Till the beginning of the present century there was no clear division between literature, religion, philosophy, and other disciplines in Tamilnadu. And so many works which are counted as literature have insignificant or even no literary value at all. Tolkappiyar, for example, is a very significant grammarian but no poet. The line of division between these disciplines is even now not sharply drawn. Thus, persons are counted as poets who are actually grammarians, philosophers, or scholars in other fields, and in the last two centuries they dealt with themes in poetical form which have no place in literature. So it is no wonder, then, that Bharati criticizes this widespread confusion of scholarship and poetical ability as a serious hindrance to the growth of real poetry. But this was not the only reason for literary stagnation. In analyzing the situation of Tamil literature of his time Bharati adds other more important facts:

"In Tamilnadu real poetry does not get its due honor. Many authors translate stories from English and many people read them. Others again write new novels of a very low standard, imitating the English pattern; they get a little profit. A few writers have appeared, who write books imbued with real literary quality and divine grace. But there is nobody to edit their works. Even when some of them are published, people do not buy them. The common people cannot appreciate the quality of a work written in a new way. The country is in such a position, that the masses follow the way shown by the English educated "heads of the society." And these are quite certain of it, that it is impossible, to find anything new and praiseworthy in Tamil works. Therefore writers, who are without any possibility to continue their work shown by God, turn to another job. The late Rajamaiyar has shown a real talent in writing Tamil stories in a new style but he did not get proper encouragement. Having no possibility to develop his ability more and more, he left this work just in the beginning and started a monthly magazine in English."[12]

In this statement Bharati illustrates some literary tendencies and efforts of his time. Many authors translated stories and novels from English and other European languages and from Bengali literature (mainly Bankim Chatterjee and Tagore) as well. Others again imitated English literature. This translating and imitating is doubtlessly a necessary step towards the formation of modern Indian literatures, considering the unequal development of various literatures of the world and the backwardness of Indian literature of that time. Bharati does not oppose imitating English and other European languages in a creative sense. This is evident from the context of his writings. We can find even in Bharati the influence of Western poets like Shelley and Walt Whitman. Bharati condemns here more the production of worthless, cheap conversion literatures (detective, adventure, love stories) patterned on English works, which were then the main books of English-educated Indians. In opposition to this he shows us the extraordinarily difficult position of those artists who made serious efforts to create a new, independent Tamil literature, for they had neither financial support nor readers.

In what did Bharati see the main reason for the stagnation of Tamil literature? He claimed that "as long as the people of a country adhere to enthusiasm for truth and to praise of heroism, a great rise of arts and sciences takes place there. In times of decay, in times of dishonor, arts and sciences do not flourish. Manliness has left us Tamilians. Heroism has gone. Our country does not belong to us. We have no freedom. Will, under these circumstances, Sarasvati descend to this country?"[13] Bharati sees the main hindrance for a free growth of modern literature in the politically outlawed and degraded condition of the Tamilians. Like Vivekananda and other philosophical and political leaders of those days Bharati is not satisfied to pillory British colonialism; he condemns more the weakness, fear, and fatalism of his own people and their consequent passivity. In order to bring Tamilnadu to a new literary and cultural renaissance he tries to revive the creative energies of the Tamils.

Already in the quotations given above Bharati hints at a few other reasons for the slow evolution of a modern literature in Tamilnadu. The new literature found neither readers nor financial support. This fact is reflected in Bharati's life too; after having left the Ettayapuram court he lived in steady material need. Only with great efforts did he succeed in publishing some of his works during his lifetime and only many years after his death did he become well-known and famous in Tamilnadu. Unlike Bengal, a strong, national-minded middle class was missing in Tamilnadu, which should have supported the new literary efforts. A part of the English-educated circles, that is, the English-educated urban sections, despised their own mother tongue and looked disdainfully at the newly developing literature. Instead of believing in the greatness and future of their own language and literature they worshipped English culture and civilization. The lowest strata of the people were uneducated and almost illiterate, and they could not give any support to the literature.

Having demonstrated some of the main reasons for the stagnation of the Tamil literature, Bharati turns to the way in which Tamil literature must be revived and developed. He writes, "In a land where outstanding personalities of the past are not remembered with reverence, there is no hope that new great ones will be born. Even if by chance a few appear there, they will not get proper estimation. If the people of a land do not admire the great of olden days, if they do not try to follow their maxims as far as possible how can they pay proper homage to new great men?"[14]

The emphasis on cultural tradition is natural among all nations fighting for their national independence. Likewise in India retrospection and glorification of her long and famous cultural past have played an important role in shaping the national consciousness. This also found its expression in literature. In his prose writings and in some of his poems Bharati himself praises the ancient culture and especially the ancient literature of Tamilnadu, and he reminds Tamilians of their two-thousand-year-old literary tradition. He wants to infuse them with pride in their ancient poets. Thus he sings in the poem "Tamil": "Among the poets we know / nobody in the whole world is born / who can be compared with / Kamban, Valluvar, Ilango." Again in "Tamilaccati" he states:

> The poetry of Silappathikaram;
> Tirukkural's soundness, clarity,
> depth of meaning, abundance and beauty,
> Kamban's efforts to show with but hints
> The limitless:
> Considering all these, I had been previously convinced,
> that the Tamil-race has obtained immortality. . . .

In those days the emphasis on the ancient literary tradition was very necessary in order to wake up the national consciousness and arouse the Tamilian's pride in their own achievements. Due to the neglect of their own literary tradition in Tamilnadu many ancient works had fallen into oblivion or had been destroyed. In the beginning of this century, U.V. Swaminatha Aiyar started to collect and publish the fragments of ancient works. Bharati himself planned a publication of ancient Tamil works with the help of others.

But it must be emphasized that Bharati never preaches the

glorification and revival of every tradition. On the contrary, he condemns those who are ready to follow implicity every tradition, good or bad, and he calls them contemptuously "fools, who drink salty water because the well was sunk by their father."[15]

Bharati wishes to revive the progressive tendencies of the ancient and of the medieval Tamil literature which could support the propagation of the national and socio-reformative aims of his time through its ideas, and which could encourage the further development of the modern literature through its artistic perfection. So he quotes and praises in many places Tiruvalluvar, Auvaiyar, the Vaishnavite and Saivaite Bhakti poets (7th-9th centuries), Kamban, Thayumanavar, and other great Tamil poets. Some of them had "a significant influence on Bharati's ideas, language and style."[16] Generally speaking it can be stated that Bharati did not merely quote these poets but used the best elements to create a modern poetry to the best of his ability.

But Bharati also recognizes that it is not enough to be proud of the past achievements. He demands new, great works from his countrymen: "New works of immortal fame / must be written in Tamil. . . . "

So he looks very attentively for every sign of the new; he mentions again and again the literary activities of U.V. Swaminatha Aiyar, Va. Ve. Su. Aiyar, Rajam Aiyar, and others. The sources for the formation of the modern literature Bharati sees in the best achievements of the ancient literature. Another mighty source for Bharati's considerations and personal experiences are the artistic creations of the people. He writes: "We see the poetic beauty in the cart-man's song, in the snake-charmer's song, in the hill womanfolk's song and in other folk-songs, though there are grammatical mistakes."[17] Bharati does not only refer others to this inexhaustible source, but he himself uses popular rhythms, metrics, proverbs, idioms, and other devices in his poetry. "The rhythms of folk-songs and drama slowly gain prominence: and Bharati has proved that they are fitting vehicles for his mystic, national and epic poetry."[18]

Bharati expresses also valuable ideas on the tasks and character of the modern literature. Thus he writes: "Now the time has gone in the whole world, when the arts and sciences relied upon kings and feudal lords. In future all arts and sciences will get nourishment and support from the common people. It is the duty of the poets to develop amongst them a real aesthetic taste."[19] With these few words he shows the change in the Tamil literature from a feudal court poetry to a literature for the broad masses. At the same time he formulates with it the aims and tasks of his own literary activity and the literary efforts of his day to create a literature understandable and clear to the people in content and form. To some of his contemporaries who feared that art may suffer a loss of quality he objects:

> The people are the kings. If you
> educate these kings,
> and give them knowledge, no loss
> will occur to the arts.[20]

In the framework of the educational efforts of that time Bharati recognizes that it is extraordinarily important to educate the masses in order to make them able to understand and to take care of the arts, of the ancient traditional arts as well as of the new, growing arts. In this connection he demands from the poets and writers that they should write good books for the education of the people. With this he underlines the social role of literature. These ideas are of great national significance because they helped to infuse national consciousness and pride in Tamil classical literature, and they encouraged the Tamilians to great efforts in this field of new literature. They are of social importance, too, because they supported the creation of a literature for the people.

Master of the twin harmonies of prose and poetry, a close student of many languages, a tireless and impassioned writer — Bharati's position in Tamil literature is unassailable. Indeed, surveying his life and work, one is struck by his inveterate optimism. In spite of penury, ill-health, and repeated frustrations, he retained his firm faith in Shakti, the Mother who was sure to save us and ensure our weal. His universal love regarded Nature as a friend. He delighted in the opulence of the five elements. The sheer exuberance of his poetry and prose is an expression of a philosophy of living, of living joyously, abjuring darkness and death. Bharati would have none of the ascetic's denial. True asceticism lies in controlling the mind. A clean mind in a clean body will think clean thoughts and engage in clean actions. For the rest, man must not make his present a hell by moodily thinking of the past or renouncing the world in disgust. The real yoga is to wring happiness out of existing circumstances, by training one's eyes on the beckoning future, and not on "the dead past":

Stumble not, fools! into the pit —
The preying, destroying recapitulation
Of things past and done with —
Nor with the agony of vain regrets.
The Past will not return!
Rather grapple to your heart the thought
That you have today achieved
Another birth.

John Cowper Powys said of Walt Whitman: "It seems to me, then, that Walt Whitman's optimism is the life-blood of his poetry, and that the boldest and most heart-satisfying mysticism ever projected by a poet's will to believe is the life-blood of his optimism."[21] These words apply to Subramanya Bharati as well. An ardent admirer of Walt Whitman, Bharati, too, wrote prose poems that triumphantly proclaim the divine that is imminent in all nature. In his ideal world there would be neither sorrow nor the canker of suspicion. Death is to be spurned like "a piece of weed." The sights and sounds of Nature are to be welcomed with joy. Our people can be assured a happy, prosperous future if we long for it and work for it. Bharati died young. Even so, he died after giving us a deathless message of courage and hope. We need have no regrets that he did not become a world figure in his lifetime. Today the world acknowledges the greatness of the man and his work.

While Tamil lives Bharati, too, shall live on the lips and in the hearts of scholars and laymen. The poet, because he is a poet, may be assured an equally enduring place "on the lips and in the hearts of all Tamils." In the words of Navaratna Rama Rao: "So long as men love motherland and goodness, so long will Bharati continue to be read. Even if he lives only as long as the glorious Tamil language, it would not be incorrect to call him immortal."[22]

Notes and References

Preface

1. C. Rajagopalachari, *The Voice of a Poet* (Calcutta, 1951), p. ix.

Chapter One

1. See Prof. Haeckel, *History of Creation,* 11, 325-26; 1, 361; and the *Pedigree of Man,* pp. 80-81, 173.
2. C. Jesudasan and Hephzibah Jesudasan. *A History of Tamil Literature* (Calcutta, 1961), p. xii.
3. J. M. Somasundaram Pillai, *History of Tamil Literature* (Annamalainagar, 1968), pp. 13-14.
4. V.R.R. Dikshitar, "Some Jain Contributions to Tamil Literature" in *Transactions of 16th All India Oriental Conference,* pp. 274-80.
5. S. K. Mukherjea, "The Golden Thread" in *Essays on Bharati* (Calcutta, 1970), III, xx-xxi.
6. S. Vaiyapuri Pillai, *History of Tamil Language & Literature* (Madras, 1956), pp. 104-105.
7. C. Jesudasan and Hephzibah Jesudasan, *A History of Tamil Literature pp. 157-85.*
8. *Ibid.,* pp. 202-31.
9. *Ibid.,* pp. 249-51.
10. Jawaharlal Nehru quoted in *Novamani* Dec. 12, 1963 [in Tamil], p. 5.
11. A.S. Raghavan, Introduction to *The Voice of a Poet* (Calcutta, 1951), p. 6.
12. C. Jesudasan and Hephzibah Jesudasan, *A History of Tamil Literature pp. 255-56.*
13. R. Rangachari, *Tamil Historical Review* published in *An Anthology of Indian Literatures* (Bombay, 1969), p. 562.

Chapter Two

1. *Essays on Bharati,* III, xxxv-vi.
2. Prema Nandakumar, *Subramania Bharati* (New Delhi, 1968), p. 7.

3. Mathuram Bhoothalingam, *The Finger on the Lute* (New Delhi, 1970), pp. 33-40.

4. Prema Nandakumar, *Subramania Bharati*, pp. 10-11.

5. V. Ramaswamy, *Mahakavi Bharatiyar* [in Tamil] (Madras, 1944), p. 127.

6. R.A. Padmanabhan, "Bharati's Associates" in *Essays on Bharati* (Calcutta, 1962), II, 17.

7. C. Rajagopalachari, *Young India*, Oct. 6, 1928.

8. Prema Nandakumar, *Subramania Bharati*, p. 26.

9. C. Subramanya Bharati, *Agni and other Poems and Translations* (Madras, 1937), p. 6.

10. R.A. Padmanabhan, *Chitra Bharati* [in Tamil] (Madras, 1957), p. 217.

11. *Parati Nulkal Nankam Pakuti, Tamilnatu Aracankam* [in Tamil] (1953), pp. 247-48.

12. Bharati, *Agni and other Poems and Translations*, pp. 32-47.

13. Chellamma Bharati, *Bharatiar Charitham* [in Tamil] (Madras, 1946), pp. 120-22.

Chapter Three

1. P.N. Appu Swami, "Introduction" to, *The Plough and The Stars* (London, 1963).

2. A.V. Subramania Aiyar, "Bharati's Religious Poetry" in *Essays on Bharati* (Calcutta, 1970), III, 76.

3. K. Meenakshisundaram, "Bharati's Poetical Works" (unpublished thesis).

4. Prema Nandakumar, *Subramanya Bharati*, pp. 68-69.

5. James H. Cousins, "Liberation" in *Agni and other Poems and Translations* (Madras, 1937), p. 15.

6. C. Rajagopalachari, "Freedom" in *The Voice of a Poet* (Calcutta, 1965), pp. 1-2.

7. Bharati, *Agni and other Poems and Translations*, pp. 11-12.

8. *Mahakavi Paratiyar Katturaikal Kalaikal* [in Tamil] (Madurai, 1962), p. 57.

9. *Ibid.*, p. 249.

10. P. Mahadevan, *Subramanya Bharati: Poet and Patriot* (Madras, 1957), p. 168.

11. *Mahakavi Paratiyar Katturaikal Kalaikal* p. 71, 249.

12. Suddhananda Bharati, *Kavikuyil Bharati* [in Tamil] (Anbu Nilayam, 1946), p. 196.

13. Bharati, *Agni and other Poems and Translations* pp. 3-10.

14. See Rabindranath Tagore, *What is Art* in *Complete Works of Rabindranath Tagore* (Calcutta, 1959), pp. 147-48.

15. S.K. Mukherjea, "The Golden Thread" in *Essays on Bharati,* III, vi.
16. K. Chandrasekharan, "Bharati's Mysticism" in *Essays on Bharati,* III, 69.
17. R. S. Desikan, "Bharati's Kannan Pattu" in *Essays on Bharati,* II, 158.
18. Bharati, *Agni and other Poems and Translations,* p. 22.
19. K. R. Srinivasa Iyengar, *Indian Writing in English* (Bombay, 1962), p. 106.
20. Prema Nandakumar, *Subramanya Bharati,* p. 107.
21. M. Ramaswamy, "Panchali's Vow — Drama? Epic?" in *Essays on Bharati,* II, 150.
22. T. P. Meenakshisundaram Pillai, "The Kuyil Song" in *Bharati Jayanti.*
23. *Ibid.*
24. Sakuntala Bharati, "My Father" in *Essays on Bharati,* II, 129-30.
25. A. V. Subramanya Aiyar, "Bharati's Religious Poetry" in *Essays on Bharati,* III, 77.
26. *Works of Bharati — Prose* (Madras, 1941), p. 140.

Chapter Four

1. Mandayam Srinivasachariar, "Preface," *Chitra Bharati* [in Tamil] (Madras, 1957).
2. *Collected Essays and Papers of Bharati* [in Tamil], IV, 151.
3. *Mahakavi Paratiyar Katturaikal. Matar* [in Tamil], p. 39.
4. Mu Varadarajan, *Tamil Literature* (Agra, 1951), p. 13.

Chapter Five

1. Exhibits 0000.1 and 0000.2 in King Emperor v. Nilakanta Bramachari published in *Madras High Court Proceedings 1911-1912.*
2. S. Sathyamurthi's speech published in *Proceedings of Madras Legislative Council* (1928).
3. *Ibid.*
4. C. S. Kamlapati, *Bharati's Blue Print for National Integration* in *Essays on Bharati* (Calcutta, 1970), III, 23-30.

Chapter Six

1. T. P. Meenakshisundaram Pillai, *Tamil Literature* (Delhi, Contemporary Indian Literature: 1957), p. 136.
2. C. Subramania Bharati, *Vinayakar Nanmani Malai, etc.* [in Tamil] (Madras, 1930), p. 142.

3. T. P. Meenakshisundaram Pillai, *Tamil Literature,* p. 147.

4. C. Rajagopalachari, "A Living Poet and Social Reformer," *Commonweal* Oct. 20, 1916.

5. R. S. Desikan, "Bharati's 'Sixty six' " in *Essays on Bharati,* III, 102-104.

Chapter Seven

1. K. Chandrasekharan, "Bharati's Mysticism" in *Essays on Bharati,* III, 68-75.

2. See *History of Western Literature* (Harmondsworth, 1950), p. 139.

3. J. Huizinga, *The Waning of the Middle Ages* (Harmondsworth, 1955), pp. 119-120.

Chapter Eight

1. T. P. Meenakshisundaram Pillai, "The Rhythm of the Common Speech — its Glorification by Bharati" in *Essays on Bharati* III, 17.

2. Swami Vivekananda, *Inspired Talks* (Madras, 1964), p. 51.

3. M. Manuel, "Bharati on the Nature of Poetry" in *Essays on Bharati,* (Caluctta, 1962), II, 2-15.

4. T. P. Meenakshisundaram Pillai, "The Kuyil Song" in *Bharati Jayanti.*

5. *Periyasami Thooran, Bharati Tamil* [in Tamil] (Madras, 1939), p. 183.

6. *Collected Essays and Papers of Bharati* [in Tamil] III, 51.

7. V. R. R. Dikshidar, *Studies in Tamil Literature and History* (Madras, 1936), p. 113.

8. V. S. Chengalvaraya Pillai, *History of Tamil Prose Literature* (Madras, 1928).

9. Mu Varadarajan, *Tamil Literature,* p. 43.

10. *Mahakavi Paratiyar Katturaikal. Kalaikal,* p. 64.

11. *Ibid.,* pp. 51-52.

12. *Ibid.,* p. 71.

13. *Ibid.,* p. 149.

14. *Ibid.,* p. 57.

15. *Ibid.,* p. 4.

16. *Ibid.,* p. 50.

17. *Parati Nulkal Namkum Pakuti . . . ,* p. 249.

18. K. Meenakshisundaram, *A Study of the Poetical Works of Subramania Bharati* (Madras, 1955), p. 133.

19. *Mahakavi Paratiyar Katturaikal Kalaikal,* p. 71.

20. *Ibid.,* p. 249.

21. V. K. Chari, *Whitman in the Light of Vedantic Mysticism* (Lincoln, 1964), p. 137.

22. C. Viswanath Iyer, *Bharati and his Works* (Madras, 1929), p. xiv.

Glossary

Amritam — Nectar

Athi — Beginning of Spring

Bharat Mata Navaratna Malai — Garland of nine gems of Mother India

Chinna Sankaran Kathai — Story of Small Sankara (Poet's autobiography)

Desiya Kidangal — National Songs

Divya Drishti — Divine sight

Janma Bhoomi — Motherland (Literally Land of Birth)

Jaya Bharata — Song of India

Kuyil Pattu — Song of the Cuckoo

Panchali Sapatham — Panchali's vow

Prabandhas — Ancient legends that deal with creation of the universe, its destruction, genealogy of the gods, etc.

Rajasuva — Horse sacrifice performed by ancient Indian Kings to commemorate their victory

Samadhi — Ecstasy, trance, complete concentration, communion with God

Samarasa — Unity of religions

Sanmarga — Good life

Smritis — Religious texts which were transmitted to others by sages who had "remembered" the substance of such texts

Swadesha Gitangal — Songs of Freedom

Vande Mataram — Hail Motherland

Selected Bibliography

PRIMARY SOURCES

Bharathi Nulkal, nankam pakuti. Tamilnatu aracankam: 1953.
Bharathi Nulkal, nankam pakuti. Tamilnatu aracankam: 1961.
Bharathi Nulkal, nankam pakuti. Tamilnatu aracankam: 1963.
Bharathi Nulkal, (vachanangal). Madras: Bharathi Press, 1930.
Chandirikaiyin Kathai. Madras: Bharathi Press, 1930.
Collected Essays & Papers. Jesudasan.
Desiya Gitangal. Madras: Bharathi Prachuralayam, 1949.
Essays - Kalaikal. Madras: Bharathi Prachuralayam, 1949.
Gnana radam. Madras: Bharathi Press, 1925.
Katchi. Madras: Bharathi Press, 1930.
Kathai Kottu. Madras: Srinagal Company.
Kuyil. Madras: Bharathi Press, 1930.
Mahakavi Bharatiyar Kavithaigal. Madras: Shakti Karyalayam, 1957.
Mathar. Madras: Bharathi Press, 1935.
Navathanthirak-kathaikal. Madras: Raman Pathippakam, 1956.
Padanjali yoga suthiram. Madras: Bharathi Prachuralayam.
Panchali Sapatham. Madras: Bharathi Press, 1930.
Pudiya athisudi, pappap-pattu, Murasu, Bharathi aruppattaru. Madras: Bharathi Press, 1930.
Samuham. Madras: Bharathi Puthaka Nilayam, 1956.
Tharasu. Madurai: Bharathi Press, 1934.
Thathuvam. Madras: Bharathi Press, 1935.
Vedantha-p-padalkal. Madras: Bharathi Press, 1930.
Vinayakar nanmani malai. Madras: Bharathi Press, 1930.
Works of Bharathi - Prose. Madras: Bharathi Prachuralayam, 1941.
Women, Essays of Bharathi. Madras: Bharathi Prachuralayam, 1941.

SECONDARY SOURCES

ANANTACHARI, AKOOR. *Kavi Chakravarthi Subramania Bharathi Charithram.* Kittappa Malar Prasuralayam Shenkottah: 1936.

APPUSWAMI, P. N. *The Plough and the stars.* London: 1963.
BHARATHI, CHELLAMMA. *Bharathiar Charitham.* Madras: Sakthi Kariya-
    layam, 1946.
BHARATHI, THANGAMMAL. *Bharathiyarum Kavithayum.* Karaikundi: Pudumai
    Padippagam, 1947.
IYENGAR, K. R. SRINIVASA. *Indian Writing in English* Bombay: Asia Publish-
    ing House, 1962.
MAHADEVAN, P. *Subramania Bharathi — A Memoir.* Madras: Atri Publish-
    ers, 1957.
MEENAKSHISUNDARAM, K. *A Study on the Poetical Works of Subramania
    Bharathi.* Madras:
–––––. *"Bharathi's Poetical Works."* Unpublished thesis.
MEENAKSHISUNDARAM PILLAI, T. P. *Tamil Literature.* Delhi: Contemporary
    Indian Literature, 1957.
–––––. "The Kuyil Song" in *Bharathi Jayanti.*
VARADARAJAN, MU. *Tamil Literature.* Agra: Indian Literature, 1951.
NANDAKUMAR, PREMA. *Bharathi in English Verse.* Madras: Higginbothams,
    1958.
–––––. *Subramania Bharathi.* Mysore: Rao and Raghavan, 1964.
PADMANABHAN, R. A. *Chitra Bharati.* Madras-18: Amuda Nilayam, 1957.
PERIASAMI, THOORAN, ed. *Bharathi Tamizh.* Amuda Nilayam, 1953.
PRABHU, R. K., ed. *An Anthology of Modern Indian Eloquences.* Bombay:
    Bharatiya Vidya Bhavan, 1960.
PRABHU, R. K., ed. *Indian National Songs.* Bombay: Popular Prakashan,
    1966.
RAJAGOPALAN AND SUNDARARAJAN. *Kannan En Kavi.* Madras: Shakti
    Karylayam, 1966.
RAMASWAMY, V. *Mahakavi Bharatiyar* Madras: Shakti Karyalayam, 1944.
REDDY, C. R. AND VENKATARAMANI, K. S. ed; *Agni and Other Poems and
    Translations.* Madras: Bharati Prachuralayam, 1937.
SASTRI, K. S. RAMASWAMI. *Subramania Bharati — His Mind and Art.* Wealth
    and Welfare Office, Madras. 1951.
SETHU PILLAI, R. P. *Bharathiar inkavi thirattu.* Madras: Palaniappa
    Brothers, 1957.
SRINIVASA RAGHAVAN, A. ed., *The Voice of a Poet.* Calcutta: Bharati Tamil
    Sangam, 1951.
SRI P. [PSEUD.] *Bharathi-Nan Kandathum kettachum.* Madras: Star
    Prasuram, 1961.
SUBRAMANIAM, K. N. ed. *Bharati.* Madras: Tamil Writers' Association, 1959.
SUDDHANANDA, BHARATI. *Kavikuyil Bharati.* Madras: Anbu Nilayam, 1948.
SUNDARAM, P. M. *Bharatiyar: Varalarum Kavithayum.* Madras: Orient
    Longmans, 1954.
VISWANATH, IYER C. *Bharati and his works* Madras: Bharati Prachura-
    layam, 1929.
YADUGIRI, AMMAL. *Bharati Ninaivukal.* Madras: Ananda Nilayam, 1954.

Index

92223

894.8
S941R

92223

AUTHOR

Roy, Kuldip K.

TITLE

Subramanya Bharati.

DATE DUE	BORROWER'S NAME